' *Congratulations on having created such a wonderful project here in the heart of Eryri.*

This is an inspiring story and shows how such initiatives are possible wherever there is determination, a sense of place and a strong connection to the local community.

I hope this book helps to spread the news throughout Wales and beyond about the potential and positive impact of social businesses. '

Liz Saville-Roberts, Plaid Cymru MP for Dwyfor Meirionnydd

Social Business in Action

Trigonos
in Eryri

Richard Grover | Judy Harris | Ros Tennyson

First impression: 2025

© Richard Grover, Ros Tennyson & Y Lolfa, 2025

This book is subject to copyright and may not be reproduced
by any means except for review purposes without the
prior written consent of the publishers.

Cover image: Jordan Christina Photography

Most photographs were taken by Richard Grover
or other members of the Trigonos team over many years
but specific acknowledgement and thanks are due to
Tom Smith (pages 64 & 65) and Emma Bartley (pages 40, 60 & 67)
whom we commissioned to take specific additional images.

ISBN: 978-1-80099-634-2

Published and printed in Wales
on paper from well-maintained forests by
Y Lolfa Cyf., Talybont, Ceredigion SY24 5HE
e-mail ylolfa@ylolfa.com
website www.ylolfa.com
tel 01970 832 304

CONTENTS

OUR INTENTIONS	7
SOCIAL BUSINESS: AN INTRODUCTION	11
STARTING POINTS	21
Earlier projects	22
Shaping our business identity	30
Finding the place	31
TRIGONOS IN ACTION	43
Location	44
Context	49
Produce	56
Décor	62
Visitors	69
Values	75
FURTHER REFLECTIONS	79
Our social business approach	82
Hospitality	89
Shared leadership	96
Lessons for others	99
EPILOGUE	104
ACKNOWLEDGEMENTS	106
REFERENCES	108

> *Until one is committed there is hesitancy, the chance to draw back, always ineffectiveness.*
>
> *Concerning all acts of initiative and creation, there is one elementary truth, ignorance of which kills countless ideas and splendid plans: that the moment one commits oneself then Providence moves too.*
>
> *All kinds of things occur to help one that would not otherwise have occurred. A whole series of events issues from the decision, all manner of unforeseen incidents, meetings, and material assistance.*

Evidence of Things Not Seen: A Mountaineer's Tale
W.H. Murray

OUR INTENTIONS

This publication has been co-written by Richard Grover, Judy Harris and Ros Tennyson, the three directors of the social business called Trigonos from 1996 to 2020. The intention is to share our experience of a social business in theory and practice, with the hope that it will encourage and inspire others to 'seize the day' and take bold steps in shaping their own versions of social businesses as a contribution to making the world a kinder, more sustainable and truly inclusive place.

Inspired by a shared interest in the social business impulse, what different experiences did we each bring that provided the foundations on which this initiative would be built?

RICHARD

My first full-time job was working for a rehabilitation project with homeless people, including those who were repeat offenders in the penal system, lived in common lodging houses or had spent much time in psychiatric hospitals or institutions for those with a learning disability (called mental handicap in those days). This became established as a charitable organisation, the Peter Bedford Trust, with John Bellers as a registered trading company to develop work opportunities. This offered those we worked with first a job and then a home that was fundamental to re-building their sense of self and self-worth.

JUDY

I moved to Norwich with my family where I started a small playgroup for the neighbourhood and then created my first really large garden. Together with other young mums, I approached Norwich City Council to ask about renting a market stall for our produce. Production increased in many new directions and our market stall became quite dynamic with dolls, toys, children's clothes, garden plants, vegetables, cakes and more. Working on the land became my life's work and my main role at Trigonos where I was able to fully explore the vital importance of the interdependence between the land and people's sense of wellbeing.

ROS

For 20 years I had a wide range of (paid and unpaid) roles that made sense to me but rather confused my parents: working in fringe theatre; running summer play schemes in Kilburn; managing a project for youngsters as an alternative to custodial sentences; setting up a community kitchen using supermarket surplus food; lecturing in theatre studies to American undergraduates studying in London; overseeing an internship programme in parliament and somehow ending up in the late 1980s as CEO of Marylebone Centre Trust (MCT), a research programme examining the potential value of integrating so-called 'alternative' medicine into NHS primary care facilities. My most useful contribution to Trigonos was, I suspect, my life-long commitment to the idea: If something doesn't exist, invent it!

We were three people with very different backgrounds, personalities and experiences who found ourselves at a particular stage in our lives (in 1996, our average age was over 50) in an extraordinary place and with an amazing opportunity to create something new and different. Whilst the wonderful setting of Trigonos as a place was (and remains) of enormous importance – as the many pictures that follow will attest – it is also the case that the emergence of Trigonos as a business depended on the combination of our past experiences, the nature of our relationship and on what Judy describes elsewhere as the wellspring of trust between us.

When it came to thinking about co-creating a project, we found that we shared the same interest in working with a social business, rather than a charitable model. To this end, we registered Trigonos (the company) as a not-for-profit entity, and Trigonos (the site) as a social business. Set up in 1996 in a small village in Gwynedd, North Wales, our social business was created to provide a residential setting where different groups of people and individual guests would feel nourished, cared for and free to pursue their particular interests.

What follows is not an official company history, though we have used our best endeavours to ensure that the facts given are correct; rather it is an emerging story that charts the path we took and seeks to capture our experiences as we individually and collectively remember them. When we started to write this, we made a commitment to being as truthful as we could be and avoid the 'sanitising' that can often happen when a decision is made to go into print.

We start with a consideration of what the term 'social business' means, and an exploration of previous initiatives we had each been involved with that informed our shared project. We then move on to explore a number of key questions including:

- How did external events align behind us to make Trigonos possible?
- What unfolded over our many years of working together?
- What was it that made Trigonos work so well?
- What have we learnt about the meaning and importance of 'hospitality'?
- How did our particular social business approach play out?
- What may be the lessons for others from this social business story?

Our focus was initially on the process of finding, managing and shaping Trigonos as a social business, and that is largely what we have done. However, it became increasingly clear that, as well as being a story about a social business in action, it is also something far more elusive: an uncovering of the power of commitment, the importance of the spirit of place, and of the evolution of a quietly significant working relationship.

We are absolutely clear that Trigonos is not for copying since that it is never possible – or desirable – to simply reproduce a successful programme of work by imitation. Rather we believe that the Trigonos story may give others the confidence to create their own initiative in their own way whatever and wherever it is.

As Goethe says:

"Whatever you can do,
or dream you can do, begin it,
Boldness has genius,
power and magic in it, do it now."[1]

---

1   This is a loose translation from Goethe's *Faust* published in German in 1808. It is much quoted and is cited by W.H. Murray (see page 6) as the couplet that most inspired him in his mountaineering adventures.

Social Business: An Introduction

What is meant by the term 'social business' and how does it differ from conventional business models? It all centres on the notion of 'profit' – in the words of former Pizza Express and C4 chair Luke Johnson:

> *"Entrepreneurs build a company to get rich. The creation of jobs is a by-product of someone starting a business."*[2]

By this definition of the driving force behind mainstream business, making a profit is of paramount importance but many would now argue that this contributes to the ever-widening gulf between the very rich (notably major shareholders and senior executives in companies) and the rest of us, creating a deep disconnection at the social level where we are no longer "a society at peace with itself, a society that can live with its conscience".[3] A more recent comment on this 'deep disconnection' comes from Rebecca Solnit writing in the *London Review of Books*:

> *"The small independent businesses that we're losing sold goods, but they also gave away for free all sorts of things that are less tangible. There might be cheaper ways to buy shampoo or better selection of envelopes online, but at an in-person store you can have a social interaction, even build a relationship with the proprietor and chat with other customers or run into a friend or neighbour. That may happen in big chains such as Starbucks – but the employees aren't likely to be around for long, the profit doesn't go back into the community and the design of the place is generic, not reflecting its environment."*[4]

When positioning a project as a business, it is easy to focus on the balance sheet to the exclusion of all other factors, but in social business, the people (those who create it as well as those who benefit) are equally important and never a 'by-product'.

There is nothing wrong, in principle, with making more than you spend – in fact making a surplus is essential to ensure the survival of any business without which there would be a risk of loss of goods, services, employment and indirect community gain, or a perpetual dependence upon grant and subsidy (always assuming that these are available). But the pursuit of profit as an end in itself corrupts the potential of business to serve a wider purpose as well as the potential of individuals becoming corrupted through greed.

Peter Drucker, regarded as a leading thinker about modern business management, challenged the idea that profit and its maximisation was the primary task of business and instead proposed the creation of customers as its purpose:

---

2   Luke Johnson, ex-chair Pizza Express, from BBC Radio 4, August 2011.
3   Martin Luther King Jr.
4   Rebecca Solnit, 'In the Shadow of Silicon Valley', *London Review of Books*, February 8, 2024.

> *"The customer is the foundation of a business and keeps it in existence. For he [sic] alone gives employment. To supply the wants and needs of a consumer, society entrusts wealth producing resources to the business enterprise."⁵*

Ignore for the moment the emphasis upon consumers and focus on the relationship between the customer and the worker producing the desired goods and services, recognising that this is one of true interdependence. They need each other. The customer needs what is produced and the worker needs to work since being in employment is commonly regarded as essential to leading a useful, purposeful and comfortable life. This is clearly still the case for most people, although it is worth noting that the idea is being increasingly challenged.

Fritz Schumacher, writing about "economics as if people mattered" in his seminal book *Small is Beautiful*, explains this understanding through what he sees as the Buddhist view of the function of work, which is:

> *"... to give a man [sic] the chance to utilize and develop his faculties; to enable him to overcome his ego-centeredness by joining with other people in a common task; and to bring forth the goods and services needed for a becoming existence."⁶*

At first sight Drucker and Schumacher may not appear to have a great deal in common but they are addressing the same key issue – the purpose of business – and coming to remarkably similar conclusions. It is all about the importance of work to the individual both in the act of producing and of using the product or service that results. Schumacher goes a stage further by examining the quality of work:

> *"To organize work in such a manner that it becomes meaningless, boring, stultifying or nerve-wracking for the worker would be little short of criminal; it would indicate a greater concern with goods than with people, and an evil lack of compassion..."⁷*

The problem is that the views of Drucker and Schumacher do not hold sway. Rather, the dominant theme is commonly that expressed by Luke Johnson: that it is all about a few people getting very rich through maximising profits and seeing employees and workers as nothing more than a necessary component. This is often said to be the price paid for following the current capitalist model that is positioned as fundamental to improving the circumstances of the wider population and guaranteeing the continuous growth deemed a necessity for business success.

So far as the organisation of business is concerned, the shareholder company model has prevailed

---

5 Quoted in *Lessons from Peter Drucker* by William Cohen.
6 *Small is Beautiful: A Study of Economics as if People Mattered*, E.F. Schumacher, 1973.

7 Ibid.

– being seen as both inevitable and optimal. However, since the collapse of banks in 2008, and extended recessions around the world, along with the increasingly casual nature of employment and growing doubts about the sustainability of continual economic growth, there has been a more rigorous questioning of the current business model. Added to this is the acknowledgement of the growing climate crisis and its huge impact on the future of the planet.

These crises fuel the enquiry into finding better ways of doing business and have led to a surge of interest in, and development of, social businesses, social enterprises, co-operatives, not-for-profits, community interest companies and the like. Whilst they account for a very small percentage of world economic activity, they give voice to a widening concern about the role of profit within businesses and their power to work against the wider common humanitarian and environmental interests.

The issue is not just about profits but also about the ownership of the business, for with ownership comes the power to sell the ownership to another party and to benefit from the sale price. The vendor is rewarded through disposition of a capital asset which has been accumulated through the efforts of all those engaged in the business. Yet the community and the company's employees generally gain nothing and lose everything. For this reason we chose to avoid all ownership issues relating to the business through the device of a legal entity that in itself was not something that had a market value.

The combination of distant shareholders who take a profit, often based on short-term gains, and the enormous sums accruing to the 'executive class', has given the idea of profit a jaded reputation. The key issue, however, is not the making of profit but rather what is involved in achieving it and how it is subsequently deployed.

When we described Trigonos (the company), we called it a 'not-for-profit social business' from the start, but what did we mean and where did Trigonos really belong? We had no clear definitions of what constituted a social business in 1996, but later found that we fitted quite well with the description given by the Social Enterprise organisation:

> *"Social enterprises are businesses that are changing the world for the better. Like traditional businesses they aim to make a profit but it's what they do with their profits that sets them apart – reinvesting or donating them to create positive social change. Social enterprises are in our communities and on our high streets – from coffee shops and cinemas, to pubs and leisure centres, banks and bus companies."*

They go on to say:

"By selling goods and services in the open market, social enterprises create employment and reinvest their profits back into their business or the local community.

This allows them to tackle social problems, improve people's life chances, provide training and employment opportunities for those furthest from the market, support communities and help the environment.

Often they're creating jobs and opportunities for those most marginalised from the workforce. It's business for good and when they profit, society profits."[8]

Later we came across the description of social business given by Muhammad Yunus, founder of Grameen Bank in Bangladesh.[9] He starts with a problem statement – namely that business is focused on the maximisation of profit and the assumption that the best impacts on society comes about when individuals look for selfish benefits. His response to this problem begins with replacing what he calls "the one-dimensional person" (i.e. someone who is solely concerned with their own profit) with the concept of the multi-dimensional person, "a person who has both selfish and selfless interests at the same time." He goes on to say that:

"The second kind of business, built on the selfless part of human nature, I have named social business. In a social business an investor aims to help others without making any financial gain himself. The social business is a business because it must be self-sustaining – that is, it generates enough income to cover its own costs."

He adds that the very purpose of such a business is to deal with major societal problems and that, although the company makes a surplus, nobody takes a dividend. He also observes that people's contributions are not limited to funding:

"People give not only money but their creativity, networking skills, technical prowess, life experience and the resources to create social businesses that can change the world."[10]

So, was Trigonos a social enterprise or a social business?

When we started, we did not spend time researching this issue, rather we created our own rules to fit the situation in which we found ourselves. Those who invested in Trigonos (the company) were a mixture of those who required a financial return (e.g. Triodos bank) and those who didn't (e.g. most of the individuals who gave us donations and loans during the setting up stage). *Continued on page 18.*

---

8 www.socialenterprise.org.uk/what-is-it-all-about/
9 *Social Business,* Muhammad Yunus, Public Affairs, New York, 2011.

10 Ibid.

One of the many additional benefits of operating as a social business is that of making connections with others in the same locality – whether these are other social businesses or small business 'start-ups'. Actively seeking such connections gives all those involved direct experience of the value of working for mutual benefit rather than competitive advantage.

This image (that we have chosen for the cover of this publication) for example, is a multi-media piece illustrating the Nantlle Ridge that runs to the South of the Trigonos site. Using spun and unspun sheep's wool and pieces of slate from the slate quarries, local artist and photographer Jordan Christina is building a small business selling her original artwork in the form of photographed greetings cards – which are available for sale in the Trigonos shop.

Image reproduced by kind permission of local artist Jordan Christina

The financial loans and gifts were very important but so were the non-financial contributions. As Yunus describes, people giving their particular skills, knowledge and enthusiasm has an enormous value in the way it provides support and endorsement without the expectation of financial return.

Perhaps it doesn't much matter what label you give your undertaking, but it does matter that those involved focus on creating a model and rules that are most likely to enable them to achieve the goals they have set, with due consideration for the context in which they will be operating.

The benefit of not being too 'purist' in our approach was that we had no qualms about, nor saw any impediment to, accepting both interest-free and interest-earning loans alongside outright donations and, at a later stage, local authority and government grants. Our financing decisions were determined by what other forms of income, in addition to the earned income from visitors, would best ensure sustainability and the holistic development of the project.

So what emerged was a hybrid financial model which offered considerable financial flexibility, minimal dependency on a sole income stream, as well as a level of security and continuity.

Our experience leads us to believe that 'social business' is a flexible term rather than a specific model. There are certain fixed factors, such as no corporate or private ownership, but, apart from these, there are many different forms of social business (or enterprise) where the decisions on the different elements are made in the light of its primary purpose and in relation to the wider environment in which it operates.

We found this approach encouraging to our somewhat bold, perhaps impulsive, experiment; satisfying too, in terms of enabling us to feel we were living purposeful and productive lives, and rewarding as others became excited by what we were doing and started initiatives of their own inspired by what they saw.

'Where so much conventional business practice is verging on the dishonest, exploitative or outright criminal and with enormous sums of money going to the very few and where there is little or no regard for the common good, then the business is operating without a sound ethical base.

As such, it is bound to fail in its wider responsibilities. Social business is founded on something completely different.'

Richard

Dawn at Trigonos

STARTING POINTS

Earlier projects

We each of us brought diverse experiences of earlier projects that gave us confidence to undertake something more ambitious than any one of us would have contemplated undertaking on our own. Each of these earlier projects (of which we describe four below, though there were more) also held significant lessons that we (often quite unconsciously) applied to our Trigonos journey.

PETER BEDFORD TRUST[11]

The Peter Bedford Trust (PBT) – a registered charity operating in London – was where Richard started his work life, first as a Community Service Volunteer and eventually taking over as Director some 10 years later.

PBT was established in 1969 to give chronically institutionalised and rootless people the chance to gain more control over their own lives, to feel that they were valued for what they had to offer and the opportunity to live in a more interdependent way. This ambition was pursued through the offer of employment, training, work opportunities, and / or housing, if wanted.

From these practical foundations, a number of subsidiary objectives followed – these were to:

- Find out how to sustain the individual's initial momentum, once it is released, and to avoid them falling back into a passive and static condition
- Encourage growth of mutual aid among participants and between participants and the wider community, in whatever ways seem practical
- Operate as a continuing experiment in the sense that all that is tried is recorded and open to assessment
- Pursue an educational function through recording and making open our experience

---

11 A report on the first 17 years in the life of Peter Bedford Trust described some principles that underpinned its endeavour and how they were implemented. This summary is based on that report.

The backbone of the Trust's approach was to understand and respond to each person's need to be valued as a contributing member of the community, without ever letting them feel that they were being 'carried' by others. The starting point was the offer of employment, which was made possible with a contract for the daily cleaning of some government offices. Since this did not suit everyone, it was followed by what were called 'work schemes'[12], which were intended to provide:

- An introduction to work practices and routines for people who had not worked in a structured way for a long time
- A basic training in skills that might then help people decide on their future work or training
- A source of long-term useful and productive activity for those unable or unwilling to seek employment, but who were willing to work within a manageable structure.

Housing was initially made possible by the provision of short-life housing using buildings that were due for demolition or for full rehabilitation at a later date. These were mainly forthcoming from the Greater London Council (GLC), an authority that was later disbanded for political reasons.

The Trust, together with John Bellers (registered as a company limited by guarantee which managed the employment and trading element of the Trust's activities), helped many people make a decent start to building new lives in the community from which they had previously been excluded.[13]

Direct link to Trigonos

This is where Richard learnt about managing a business, dealing with business planning, budgeting, employing, supporting employees and the importance of giving everyone a chance.

Lessons for Trigonos

- The impact of the decision to set up the business part of the operation as a company limited by guarantee and not a shareholder company or a charity
- The way it was possible to create employment for people who felt marginalised and the importance of building opportunities for supporting people's sense of self-worth
- As an employer, seeking to 'accompany' employees in their work and build on their strengths, rather than simply directing them to do their job

---

12 Such schemes included: gardening, furniture repairing, catering and office services.

13 For more background on the thinking behind the Peter Bedford Trust see *Working on Self-Respect – Writings on Offenders and other Homeless People* by Michael Sorensen, Peter Bedford Trust, 1986. (ISBN 0 948084 02 2)

HARGRAVE PROJECT

One of the things that Richard learnt from his time with the Peter Bedford Trust was how difficult it can be for people coming out of institutional care to feel welcomed and integrated into the wider community. It could be a huge jump to move from full-time care (with its limitations and frustrations) to living on your own and looking after yourself with minimal support in often quite challenging environments.

The Hargrave Project consisted of three houses – two refurbished as flats housing eight people, and the third a new-build communal house designed to house up to 14 people. The first group of residents in the shared house comprised 11 adults and three children. This 'campus' provided a home for people with very different characteristics, including some with a learning disability; with a history of mental health issues; having been homeless; experiencing personal challenges and others with no immediate apparent support needs, but wanting to live in a more inclusive and integrated way.

The children brought much to the house and to the lives of those who normally would not have had the chance to know young people so easily. In turn, the children had the opportunity to get to know a far wider group than they would have done in a more conventional family setting and all three grew up to be accepting and non-judgmental in their response to people whom others may have spurned.

There were specific features in the design of the house that carefully combined shared facilities with private space in ways that would support a sense of purposeful interdependence alongside respect for each individual's personal needs and tastes. Conversations with the architects were frustrating and amusing in equal measure. Having to make the case for large investment in internal sound insulation, for example, so that residents would not be irritated by noise from others – and the case for not having a dishwasher so that those who were not able to take on external jobs had the opportunity for purposeful activities well within their capability and valued by others.

Similarly, those in the housing association managing the project couldn't understand why we (Richard and Ros) preferred to pay rent as equal

Our House by Ricky, aged 5

People in our house by Tessa, aged 7

tenants rather than be paid to be carers for others in the house. Our rationale was that if we had been paid it would have changed the nature of the relationships and reduced the sense of equity within the resident group. This model (once the building costs had been covered) paid its way and did not need further subsidy whilst providing a safe and comfortable home for all those who lived in it.

Direct link to Trigonos

This experience of shared living confirmed our belief in the power of creating new models to fill gaps and explains our enthusiasm for Trigonos as an experiment where people, like our fellow residents in the Hargrave Project, were included and warmly welcomed.

Lessons for Trigonos

- When necessary, it is important – and possible – to challenge and change the status quo
- Projects can benefit from having a multiplicity of purposes
- A purposeful way of life can be more important than being paid

PARTNERSHIPS FOR DEVELOPMENT

The year 1992[14], saw the start of a global movement aimed at building intentional collaboration between the private sector (business), the public sector (government) and the not-for-profit sector (voluntary/non-statutory organisations). In due course, multi-stakeholder partnering was seen as the key to delivering the UN's 16 Sustainable Development Goals – it was defined as the 17th 'goal', but in fact it was an approach that underpinned the other 16.

Coinciding with her move to Wales, Ros began a 30-year involvement in exploring and promoting tri-sector partnerships for development. Not convinced by the rhetoric and the extravagant claims made for partnering, she did her best to uncover what such intentional collaboration might actually involve. She quickly discovered that, whilst every partnership was highly contextual in character and therefore unique, the process of building a partnership was remarkably cross-cultural and transferable.

Over time (and running in parallel to her involvement with Trigonos), Ros, together with a growing global network of colleagues, worked with groups and organisations ranging from the very local and informal (e.g. rural communities in Bangladesh) to the international and institutional (e.g. the World Bank in Washington).

Key to this work was the emergence of five partnering principles that seemed critical to being able to challenge and breakthrough disabling assumptions, behaviours and systems. These were:

RELISHING DIVERSITY – Seeing differences as a prompt to think and act in new ways

EQUITY – Recognising everyone's right to be at the table and their unique contribution

TRANSPARENCY – Being open about motivation, priorities and values

MUTUAL RESPECT – Giving space to knowing others and co-evolving ways of working

COURAGE – To speak truth to power and to continuously strive for better solutions

When Trigonos began, Ros's international partnering work was in its relatively early stages, but it was starting to have influence and impact and, although (apart from the personal link through Ros) it was quite separate from Trigonos, the sense of Trigonos being connected to a global movement was encouraging and important.

Direct link to Trigonos

Trigonos was the setting for the first experimental training programme for 'partnership brokers' that

---

14 This was the year of the Rio Earth Summit that, for the first time, brought business into the sustainable development debate. It was also the year Richard and Ros moved to Wales.

The 2030 Sustainable Development Goals were adopted by all United Nations members in 2015

has subsequently grown into an international phenomenon.[15] Trigonos has been described by several in that initial group as the 'spiritual home' for the partnership brokering movement.

Lessons for Trigonos
- The importance of a threefold conceptual framework
- That how you do things is as important as what you do – process really matters
- How principled ways of working are central to creating a more just and sustainable world

---

15 By 2020, some 4,000 people across the globe and from all sectors had been trained – for more information, see: www.partnershipbrokers.org

CENTRE FOR LIVING ART AND SCIENCE (CLAS)

This started as a project to provide an upper school for children from the Snowdonia Waldorf School that was, till then, only able to offer primary level education. A purpose-built timber building was constructed sitting on stilts in a sloping woodland space. It consisted of one large communal room with two medium-sized rooms – originally intended to be classrooms but which became dormitory accommodation for visiting groups. Doors from each room opened onto a balcony that went all around the outside of the building offering different views of the surroundings.

The costs were kept low because the school already owned the land and virtually all the work was undertaken by parents (amongst whom were builders, carpenters, plumbers and electricians). But without a patron (also a parent), who gifted the funds to purchase the building materials and equipment, it would never have happened.

CLAS was sparingly furnished, making it very flexible and pretty resilient to the exuberance of the young people who came to stay with their teachers on study visits. Even when groups of older people came to stay, the rather basic style of the living arrangements seemed to be acceptable because the setting was so beautiful and because something about the space seemed to encourage a feeling of community.

One feature was the way the kitchen was linked to the main meeting room through the upper half of the connecting wall being open – a kind of indoor window without glass. This meant that the groups could smell the appetising food whilst it was being prepared, and that Judy, as the main chef, could almost unconsciously, but to great effect, adjust the menu in response to the mood and tone of the group.

When emotions were running high, she would prepare food that was heavier to calm things down, or when the mood was sluggish, she would add more spice to liven things up. This was a fine example of how providing services can, at its very best, be quite an intuitive process, and laid the groundwork for the approach to the preparation and serving of healthy nourishing food that became (and remains) an important feature for those who stay at Trigonos.

A huge amount of time and effort went into creating this space that led to quite a level of disappointment when it proved impossible to sustain the upper school that had been its intended purpose. But with the change of use, the income generated from visiting groups did help to ensure the financial viability of the lower school for a good few years.

Starting Points

CLAS – Building in process

These are four very different projects but they have some qualities in common including:

- Being based on identifying a gap in existing provision
- Turning a challenge into an opportunity
- A willingness to question rules and conventional thinking
- The way they each integrated people from very different backgrounds
- Being created/co-created as an act of shared leadership

Direct link to Trigonos

CLAS was, effectively, the prototype for Trigonos – both the company and the project. It was the place that brought the three of us together around a practical project and gave us the confidence that we could undertake something more ambitious and more permanent.

Lessons for Trigonos

- Being ready to adapt as and when necessary
- The importance of patrons and patronage
- The interplay between hosting and being hosted

Shaping our business identity

From the start one thing that felt important was to give our initiative (as yet undefined) a name. We initially tried to find a Welsh name, but quickly abandoned the idea as being inappropriate since we were not Welsh speakers and it would have suggested something that was not true.

We then looked for a name that reflected a sense of the three-fold nature of our intentions – the simultaneous and interrelated pursuit of social, personal and economic development. It was not easy since many companies registered in the Isle of Man (with its flag of a 'triskelion', an arrangement of three legs) had already registered names that referenced the concept of three. Until, at one of our meetings, Judy shared a remarkable photograph of an ancient Celtic disc with three spirals emanating from a central core and suggested that this might be a 'motif' for our project.

Eventually, and after consulting a thesaurus and a dictionary, we decided on 'Trigonos' from the Greek, meaning 'a three-sided figure', in other words, a triangle. For us this was the name that best encapsulated the threefold nature both of the Celtic triskele that we had adopted as a kind of logo for the company and our growing commitment to a threefold approach to the project.

The day after we settled on the name, Ros found a stained glass image of a triskele in a nearby craft shop. This was typical of the type of occurrence described by W.H. Murray (on page 6) – the first of many – and which we came to recognise and name as a 'Murray event' because it seemed as if 'providence was moving too'.

So this version of the triskele became our logo, and the name Trigonos, always reproduced in a font known as Kells because of its Celtic associations, became the name of our registered company as well as the name of the site we eventually purchased.

Finding the place

We started our search by contacting local estate agents and going through their lists of properties. We were limited through not having a clear picture of what we wanted and not having a proper idea of what funds we could raise for purchase and the likely costs of renovating and converting a property.

We spent a lot of time travelling around north-west Wales looking at properties that in every case seemed wholly inappropriate to our purpose. This included number of small farms with many agricultural outbuildings and usually a reasonably-sized farmhouse. However, the agricultural buildings were generally in a very poor state of repair and we thought the conversion costs would be impossibly high. The farmhouses might have been big enough to accommodate our families, but not to provide the space we would need for visiting groups and activities.

After several months of looking, we were told about a place in the Nantlle Valley – about 10 miles south of the historic city of Caernarfon – by a friend and fellow parent from the Snowdonia Waldorf School. This had been converted into a commercial residential arts centre but the business had gone bankrupt a couple of years earlier. The main building, Plas Baladeulyn[16] (known locally as The Plas) had been built as the home for the manager of the local Pen yr Orsedd slate quarry in around 1865, but when the quarry closed in the 1960s the Plas and the site had been used for other purposes.

The whole site, with an uninterrupted view across the lake (Llyn Nantlle Uchaf) to the west face of Yr Wyddfa (Snowdon) was a stunning location with some very special qualities. We had not been looking for anything exceptional, but here we found ourselves in a place of dramatic beauty with a sense of both history and mystery.

In addition, the premises provided all the facilities that we required – and far more. Not a derelict barn or an unconverted pigsty in sight, but a collection of reasonably well-maintained buildings that included:

- A two-storey main house with 11 bedrooms, a large dining room with a full complement of tables and chairs, a fully equipped kitchen and two lounges
- A single-storey converted agricultural building that contained a large gallery, two other meeting rooms, a big studio and eight further bedrooms
- A two-storey converted stable block with four bedrooms

---

16   The word 'Plas' in Welsh means the large house or manor house.

Lake at sunset

In addition, there were 18 acres of land, including small woodland areas, running from the road to the lakeside and a small stream running through the centre of the property from the disused slate quarry, down to the lake and from the lake eventually running to the sea as the River Llyfni (Afon Llyfni).

The vendors were seeking to recover as much of the debt as possible that was owed by the arts centre at the point of bankruptcy, and the asking price was £320,000, which was far beyond our reach. Despite this, the place had such a sense of being right that we began to seriously think through how we might raise the funds to make this idea a reality.

The estate agency was based in Birmingham and specialised in the sale of commercial properties. The site was being marketed as a possible commercial hotel – in an area where hotels were plentiful and not necessarily flourishing – this explained why we had not come across this property when trawling through the sales lists of local estate agencies.

The agent's representative travelled up to meet with us and brought with him a collection of plans showing the buildings in detail. He seemed tired and irritated by his long journey and was quite listless whilst showing us round. We ended our tour by asking him if he could send us copies of the plans and whether we could come back to see the site again. He responded by simply handing over the plans, saying that we should return them if we decided not to make an offer. He seemed to have some confidence that we would be going ahead, even though we didn't think we had given him any reason to make that assumption. Or he may simply have not relished the idea of having to drive back to North Wales.

In any event, we saw this as another indication that 'providence was moving our way'. The agent also informed us that we could contact a local person who had basic caretaking responsibilities for the site whilst it was empty as and when we wanted further access to the buildings.

We left after our first visit debating whether this site – at least three times larger than anything we had looked at so far and requiring us to be far more ambitious in our thinking – was in any way feasible. Was the very special quality of the place enough to give us the courage and confidence to proceed?

On our next visit we were escorted by the local key-holder, with whom we made a good connection. So much so that, to our great surprise and without us making a request for further access, she gave us the keys, simply asking us to return them if we decided not to proceed with the purchase. This enabled us to have uninterrupted visits whenever we wanted to, which we made frequently over the next few weeks – bringing others with us to see their reactions to the place – and to gauge the viability of this potentially huge expansion of our plans.

Neither the estate agent nor the local key-holder seemed to be expecting much interest in the property from anyone else. In fact, they both seemed quite relaxed about the idea of us as the new owners, although why we would want the place was clearly somewhat baffling, since we were clearly not thinking of running a commercial hotel.

We felt increasing excitement at the number of external episodes ('Murray events') that seemed to confirm our growing sense that this was 'the place', and at this point we started to meet more seriously and regularly as directors-in-waiting. An early decision was to set up a company to pursue our emerging objectives. We looked through various models to be sure we were making the best choice and settled on a 'company limited by guarantee' and used the model rules provided by the Industrial Common Ownership Movement (ICOM).

It was never our intention to become a co-operative as such, but the ICOM model rules for non-profit organisations met our requirements in many ways including, most importantly, avoiding individual or corporate ownership. If we succeeded in buying the property, we were clear that it should remain forever outside corporate and private ownership and stay in the world of social business and not-for-profit organisations. We, as directors, would be acting as stewards or guardians on behalf of a public good rather than owners. This, as we saw it, was at the heart of any 'social business'.

Having found the name and started the process of registering the company, we turned our attention to raising the money needed to buy the property. Our outline plan was to seek a loan from Triodos bank[17] and to raise other loans and gifts from individuals we knew who had voiced support for our intentions.

We made an offer to the agent of £200,000 (subject to contract), which was accepted, somewhat to our surprise, given how far short of the asking price it was, but then they had been trying to sell the property for two years with no success.

To enable Triodos bank to make the decision about whether or not to grant us a mortgage, we were required to produce a business plan to demonstrate the financial viability of our project. We did this whilst being very aware that there were so many questions about the project to which we simply didn't have answers. Would self-organising groups find our setting and approach attractive? What courses could we run ourselves and who might come to them? How long would it take to build up the business to the point of sustainability?

---

17 Triodos Bank's mission is to help create a society that protects and promotes quality of life for all – www.triodos.co.uk/about-us

Plas from the front

Would we have the funds to support the endeavour through its initial development period?

Our annual income estimates were based on lettings to paying guests, running and hosting courses and, to some extent, on the income generated by two of us from our external work. In practice, this became income generated by Ros alone, since Richard's London-based work had come to an end in the interim, which was in some ways fortunate since his full-time effort was needed at Trigonos as we opened for business.

All of our financial projections were highly speculative, perhaps more speculative than the bank and our other financial supporters fully realised. However, whilst our plan may have been somewhat sketchy, we did have some credibility from the fact that two of the three of us had successfully run not-for-profit organisations prior to this and had sound financial and organisational management track records. After meeting with the bank's representatives and several re-drafts of the business plan, it passed muster.

The appeal to friends and family for gifts and loans was launched. The estate of one of the founder's family members, who had recently died, donated £25,000 to help launch the fund and this was followed by a range of gifts and interest-free loans totalling £55,000.

We could offer little by way of guarantees to those

Plas from the back

who contributed, and we felt quite overwhelmed but also moved and encouraged at the generosity and trust people showed, which was based mostly on their existing relationship to one or other of us. These donated funds contributed not just to the purchase of the property but also provided the financial cushion we needed to meet the running costs during the setting up and early operating period.

Once we had secured the additional finance necessary to proceed, Triodos Bank arranged a full valuation of the property for the purpose of assessing the mortgage. To our astonishment, the valuation came in at £160,000. Well below the figure we had offered to the vendor's agent.

We explained to the agent that we would not be able to proceed at the figure we had offered since our mortgage depended on purchasing the property at no more than the formal valuation figure. This, of course, did not please him and he said he would have to discuss our revised offer with the vendors. We waited a very uncomfortable couple of weeks, feeling that we may have lost the property and resigning ourselves to possibly starting our search again.

When, eventually, the agent phoned us it was to ask if we could offer a little more – say a further £10,000. Richard, who answered the call, stated firmly that £160,000 was our final offer and the agent, almost without taking breath, immediately accepted. So we closed the deal at what seemed a ridiculously low price and pressed ahead to completion.

Sometime later we realised that a factor that actually worked to our advantage was the presence at the centre of the site of a small cottage in which the former owner of Plas Baladeulyn still lived. It seems highly likely that potential purchasers considering the place as a commercial hotel would have been put off by this fact, whereas we only saw it a mild inconvenience.

As yet another unexpected confirmation that our project was on track, a few days after we moved into Plas Baladeulyn, a British Telecom engineer (who was a first-language Welsh speaker) arrived to connect the telephones in the office. He asked why we had chosen the name Trigonos for the business. We explained that we wanted a name that reflected a sense of three-folding. He then told us that *Trig-y-nos* was Welsh for 'staying the night'. What he actually first said was that it meant 'abiding' in the night which we found suitably poetic and appropriate for a residential retreat! We were delighted, but perhaps not entirely surprised, that our chosen name should also inadvertently have a Welsh meaning.

The process from first seeing the property to the purchase took six months but finally we took possession of Plas Baladeulyn and the surrounding land with the three of us and our three children moving in on the following day. Trigonos, the place, was born!

Trigonos entrance with sign

'June 7, 1996, was the day we moved in to what became Trigonos and recognised with an equal mix of excitement and trepidation that it was now a fact, this beautiful site and buildings were now in our care.

The 'what' and the 'why' we understood, the 'how' was to be discovered.

We three people, with our very different personalities, experiences and capacities, had to build from what we knew and find a way of working for a common purpose in order to do something useful.'

Judy

TRIGONOS IN ACTION

Location

Dyffryn Nantlle (the Nantlle Valley), which is the only true east/west valley in Eryri (Snowdonia), is the setting for one of the stories of the Welsh epic known as *The Mabinogi* or, less correctly, *The Mabinogion*[18]. The importance of *The Mabinogi* as a record of early myth, legend, folklore, culture and language is immense, and the fourth branch of *The Mabinogi* is strongly linked to the Nantlle Valley. The Arthurian legend also has a presence in the valley as it is seen as one of the sites where Arthur and his knights lie sleeping as they await the call to come to Britain's aid whenever it might be necessary.

The site is undoubtedly a place of mystery which many feel when there, even if they are not aware of the cultural history.

Alongside the ancient myths and legends, there is also the more recent rendering of the view across the lake to Snowdon captured in a painting by Richard Wilson, the 18th-century landscape painter (see page 45).

Nowadays, as you look to the right from the view across the lake to Yr Wyddfa (Snowdon), you see the Nantlle ridge and carrying on further round you see the waste heaps from the local slate quarries of Pen yr Orsedd and Dorothea. Thus, with your eyes you pass from the myths and legends, through the romantic landscape to the reality of slate waste in a devastated, post-industrial landscape. This is also part of what makes Trigonos a spectacularly striking place – the juxtaposition of beauty and harshness.

Arriving at Trigonos means passing this view of the slate quarries, visitors were often surprised that there was no gate at the entrance, no precise definition of where Trigonos started and stopped. The second thing that may have struck them was a rather scruffy car park that was not very inviting and two Gwynedd Council brown plastic bins just at the bottom of the drive!

It was not intentionally unwelcoming, it was just the way it was and perhaps it suggested that things at Trigonos were not done for show. This casual approach to the look of the place also had its merits. When visitors arrived for the first time and turned left beyond the car park and moved into the landscape; or if they had arrived at night and opened their bedroom curtains; or came into the dining room in the morning, and saw the view across the lake, then suddenly they just knew why they had come.

---

18   *The Mabinogion,* Everyman's Library 2001.

Lake in the mist

Richard Wilson painting
Courtesy National Museums Liverpool,
Walker Art Gallery

Looking across the lake past Trigonos to the slate tips

"Throughout our time at Trigonos, we found the landscape absorbing and an endless source of inspiration and discovery. Comments from visitors repeatedly confirmed their own deep gratitude and pleasure from being in this environment: watching the changing colours and the unreliable yet often exciting weather patterns.

And, of course, the magnificent rainbows that arch across from one end of the lake to the other.

Quite simply, it is a wonderful place to be."

Ros

Context

Any context is as much about the current realities for people and communities as it is about location, culture and history. As Richard describes below, this was a particularly important and sensitive issue:

> *"A significant factor was that we were incomers and English, who were now living in a strongly Welsh and Welsh-language area. We tried to explain who we were and what we were hoping to do, but it was not easy since our model of work and our aspirations were unfamiliar and some were suspicious of our motives, giving rise to a low level of local hostility for our first few years."*

This took us a little while to fully understand but, meanwhile, we were caught up in the beauty of the place, its history and our sense of responsibility to be good stewards of both.

The mountainous heartland of north-west Wales was, until the 19th century, a remote area whose communication by land with the outside world was restricted by the difficult topography. The sea had provided the most convenient means of communication in and out of the region for many hundreds of years.[19] The economy was dominated by subsistence agriculture and most buildings were constructed of stones picked out of nearby fields or quarried from nearby outcrops.

In the Nantlle Valley there was an abundance of slate. The use of slate from the valley can be traced back to the third century CE when it probably provided the roofing materials for the Roman fort at Caernarfon (known as Segontium) and a Roman bathhouse at Tremadog.

As the industry expanded from the 18th century onwards to meet the market demands for the new industrial towns and cities in Britain and, increasingly, overseas, demand for labour in the quarries grew.

By the 1860s the demand for roofing slates was so great that there was a four-year waiting list for delivery on orders. More people from the surrounding agricultural districts abandoned farming for better wages in the slate quarries, and for the improved living conditions on offer. By the late 1870s the workforce in the Nantlle Valley slate industry peaked at around 3,500 people.[20]

No longer was the valley an agricultural backwater but a very dusty and noisy district in which to live. Perhaps most important in the long run was that it brought together a critical mass of young Welsh speakers who moved from working in remote agricultural settings into newly-built settlements

---

19 The early explorers of the land routes include George Borrow, *Wild Wales,* 1862 and Thomas Pennant, *A Tour in Wales,* 1778.

20 Jones, G.P., *The Heritage of Slate in the Nantlle Valley,* Trigonos publication.

creating vibrant and densely populated communities in which the Welsh language was the bedrock of cultural activities.

By 1896, most of the inhabitants of the Nantlle Valley were employed in the industry, but production declined slowly in the early twentieth century and more rapidly in the second half. By the early 1970s both the local quarries had closed. Pen yr Orsedd re-opened in 2007 to produce crushed rock aggregate from piles of waste slate to use in road-building and urban gardens, but it only provided work for a few people.

The loss of the quarries meant a major loss of employment that was not compensated for by government investment (as had been the case in South Wales with the loss of the coal mining industry – a cause of considerable local resentment). One growth area in employment was in the hospitality sector but, since this is essentially seasonal, it didn't offer year-round employment, as had the quarries. Young people, who left school with few qualifications, faced a life of economic hardship and those who moved into higher education left the area to seek better opportunities in the towns and cities of Wales, England and further afield.

Another consequence of the growth associated with the quarries was that a very high proportion of the housing in the locality was constructed without modern amenities and with materials that provided poor insulation and allowed damp ingress, leaving the current occupiers facing high bills for heating and maintenance. Some limited attempts have been made to retrofit the old housing stock and to bring domestic buildings up to near-modern standards.

There has also been a significant increase in the number of second or holiday homes in all the local villages that has presented a challenge to the Welsh language and culture as well as making housing unaffordable for many local people.

It could easily be missed, with so much beauty, that this part of North Wales is one of the most economically under-privileged areas in the UK and was in receipt of a high level of social funding from the EU for many years. This remains the case today, but now without the EU money.

It was assumed that we (as the founding directors) must be the owners of the newly-acquired site. Local people simply could not understand that this was not the case, that we were not driven by a profit-making motive and that we would not simply sell up once we could make significant financial gain. It seemed hard for many to grasp that although we were totally in charge of a large property, we were not personally wealthy.

There is an interesting episode that illustrates how this played out in our early interactions with people in the village. During the two years when the place had been empty, people from far beyond the village, with many travelling from England, had regularly walked through the site in order to fish in the lake and nobody stopped them. Once we moved in, we explained that this would no longer be possible because it would disturb our guests. We made it clear that those who lived in the local villages would be welcome to continue fishing if, for access, they used the permissive right of way running from the road directly by the side of the lake, and as long as they had a fishing licence that we would be happy to issue to them.

This caused immediate resentment, as local fishing people assumed that we would charge a hefty fee for the licence, until we explained that the licence would be free and that its sole purpose was to assure them, as local people, of their entitlement and to ensure that there were some rules that would need to respected. The rules were simple: to leave the place as they found it (i.e. no litter, no fires) and that there should never be more than two people fishing from our shore at any one time. They came to accept that we intended the licence to be a privilege for local people and not a means to keep them out or a ploy to make money.

Misunderstandings with local people diminished quite quickly once we started engaging local youngsters to work with the catering or hospitality teams. We trained our colleagues and treated them well by: paying a decent wage (exceeding that required by the new national minimum wage legislation); never using zero hours' contracts and always offering encouragement rather than judgement or criticism. Their experiences from working at Trigonos were taken back to their families and the atmosphere with our neighbours gradually warmed.

We invited a Welsh teacher to come and give us lessons in the hope we could develop a reasonable level of confidence in the language. One of us made real progress in this, the other two didn't. But what we found was that our employment practices turned out to be of far more importance to local people than our linguistic skills and they seemed to accept our limitations with the language.

At Trigonos, we hosted an increasing number of visitors from across the globe as well as from around the UK. However, because of the lack of a common meeting place in the village, not even a shop or a pub, the connection between our guests and local residents was largely limited to those who worked with us.

Some of our guests came to feel strongly attracted to the place and to consider moving locally in order to be able to work with us. When we began to employ people at a more managerial and specialist skill level, we engaged at least four people from England who had first come to Trigonos as guests. However, none lasted very long as employees, as they (and we) quickly came to realise that they had come with a highly idealised picture of life at Trigonos and once they experienced the relative isolation and some of the challenges of living in North Wales, they decided to leave.

We did successfully employ several people of English origin in a range of roles and welcomed the experiences they were able to bring, but they were already living and had established roots in Wales long before they found us.

Over time our local employees – as well as their partners and families who had been sceptical about us when we first arrived – grew to see Trigonos as a place of hope and a stepping-stone to new opportunities. This is well illustrated by the fact that staff moved quite easily into other good jobs despite the fact that when they had started working with us many had few qualifications and, all too often, a low level of confidence and self-worth.

We couldn't be regarded as anything other than incomers because, in the context of the Nantlle Valley, that's exactly what we were, which was why we had rejected the idea of choosing a Welsh name for Trigonos because it could have given a false impression. Having acknowledged that, it is also the case that we did achieve an acceptance by the local community that was rooted in how we went about our business and most notably, in the way we worked with local people. The context of any enterprise is never static, it evolves both as a result of external changes as well as through the actions and influence of the enterprise itself.

Aerial view of the Nantlle Valley

Aerial view of the buildings

Produce

The 18 acres of land attached to Plas Baladeulyn was of enormous importance in the totality of what Trigonos became. In addition to its spectacular beauty as well as the geology, history and mythology that has shaped it, the site is at the same time both mysterious and practical.

The mystery comes from the ever-changing light, the impact of the weather on the lake, the sun that can turn the valley into a golden chalice and the way the patterns of rain and mist both obscure and then reveal the landscape. This is something over which, of course, we had no control but that many appreciated.

The pathways down to the lake and around the gardens provided the perfect opportunity for guests to take exercise, meditate or simply wander and wonder at their leisure.

The practical, however, was quite a different matter over which we (or rather, Judy) had to adopt a determined stance to bring it back from its state of waist-high brambles (in the walled garden) and the fact that there seemed to be more stone than earth in the fields that we were relying on to be productive. The intention being both to restore the environment which had been deeply depleted and to produce fruit, vegetables and herbs for use in the kitchen and, when available, for families in the surrounding villages.

For reasons of safety and to let in more light, a number of trees were taken down around the Plas, the brambles were uprooted and new beginnings were made. The initial ground clearance and fencing of fields was undertaken with groups of young people from an organisation called Drive for Youth (DfY), and we have them to thank for re-instating the traditional-style slate fencing around the oak wood and for helping to build some raised beds in the walled garden where we could start our vegetable-growing.

Our food policy made clear that we would always try to supply as much produce as possible from our own land. This we achieved in part, but we also discovered it is one thing to grow the produce and another to ensure the chefs made the best possible use of it. Most chefs produced great meals that were much appreciated by our guests but didn't give equal attention to working with seasonal and local produce. They needed to be nimble enough to incorporate what was available, adapting their recipes to take account of what was to hand even if it meant being less exotic, whilst also being aware of what other chefs might need as there was sometimes an over-demand from the kitchen.

If you are a sheep farmer and require silage for winter fodder, a flat field is not to be overlooked. So it was with ease that we slipped into a 'barter economy' with our neighbouring farmer soon

Judy's schematic for the land

after our arrival. He grazed his sheep on Trigonos land and took a summer crop of silage/haylage, which meant that our other two fields were managed in a way we would have been unable to undertake ourselves and we had a regular supply of farmyard manure for our vegetables.

For a period of time, we connected with Tai Eryri, a local housing association, to create a project to help encourage healthy eating and vegetable growing in the Nantlle Valley. We offered evening classes in basic gardening skills and were able to give practical help to a few novice gardeners at the same time, making more friends and contacts in the locality.

A Drive for Youth group in the walled garden

This led to a valuable social project (Llysiau Lleu) that started as a vegetable box scheme whereby, from our own surplus, we supplied over 20 families with a weekly box of veg. In time, this metamorphosed into a market stall in the neighbourhood community centre that was quickly joined by other stall-holders offering home baked goods, crafted items and more. It became quite a social focus every Friday, with tea and cakes available, and gave us the opportunity to pass time within the local community.

As Judy observed:

"The term 'local produce' meant more than just a label. Living in this landscape and walking daily up and down the fields over the years, something rises up through the soles of your feet to the soul of your being, something that has an ancestry and intimacy to it that helps override the difficulties of cultivation (the prevalence of stones and the tendencies of this soil to either bake or soak). Or is it just stubborn determination not to be beaten?"

An interesting addition to the land work was a project with the Sarvari Research Trust with its origins in Hungary. This organisation breeds new, disease-resistant varieties of potato. At its core was one of the UK's leading experts on potato blight who had retired as a lecturer and researcher in Genetics and Plant Pathology at Bangor University in 2002 to begin the work that led to the formation of the Trust. In order to establish their resistance to blight, the potatoes had to be grown on land that had not been used for potatoes for many years. The Trigonos land met the requirements and for three years we grew potato crops on organic principles as part of the experiment that would play its small part in building greater global food security.

In due course, a soft fruit area and a small orchard were also planted, again with the produce

destined mainly for our kitchen, and then we had chickens running around in the orchard with possibly the smartest purpose-built chicken shed in Wales.

We always avoided the use of chemical controls and inputs against pests and weeds, preferring to use organic and biodynamic[21] methods to the best of our ability. However, given the lack of understanding and acceptance of the system by some in the land team, the labour-intensive nature of the work and the lack of financial resources within Trigonos to support this, it was not possible to fully achieve that goal. There was a heavy toll on a few dedicated people, but it was remarkable how much healthy and varied produce we managed to grow.

Moving the vegetables into the field, and eventually acquiring three polytunnels, increased productivity significantly and also released the walled garden to be turned into a wonderful flower garden that was developed and managed by Judy with the help of a few dedicated and some occasional volunteers. It became a space much valued by visitors, as a place to walk or to just sit quietly and feel refreshed. The walled garden also became a space for growing herbs and providing the

---

21 Biodynamics is rooted in the work of philosopher and scientist, Rudolf Steiner, whose 1924 lectures to farmers opened a new scientific understanding with a recognition of spirit in nature. They can be applied anywhere food is grown, with thoughtful adaptation to scale, landscape, climate and culture.

Raised beds in the polytunnel

cut flowers used to decorate the public spaces and bedrooms (see pages 72 and 73).

It was always clear to us that the land is intrinsic to the whole atmosphere of Trigonos. The buildings without the land would in some ways be quite soulless. The land without the buildings would lack purpose. Truly they belong to each other, it is a marriage of necessity where joining together produces something of much greater value than either could offer independently.

Décor

We inherited buildings that had been mostly modernised to a reasonable standard, with a number of what would have been outbuildings converted into study bedrooms and a range of meeting rooms. Public rooms included a large studio with a wall of windows looking down to the lake and an impressive gallery that could be accessed directly from the car park, making it available for open events without participants having to intrude on things going on elsewhere on the site.

Whilst looking good, the buildings were unnecessarily heavy in their environmental impact. Over time, we had all the roof spaces insulated with natural materials, solar panels installed and we moved our main source of heating from oil to wood chip, requiring us to build a special boiler house (the modern structure in the lower part of the centre of the picture (see page 55).

Perhaps one of the most significant factors about the buildings at Trigonos was that guests were obliged to go out of doors in order to move from one part of the site to another. This meant regular exposure to the landscape (and the weather!), in sharp contrast to being lodged in one large building that provides for all your needs and discourages you from relating to the outside world.

The continuous interplay between internal and external experience was important – even if sometimes a little inconvenient.

So what about the internal spaces and the décor?

To many of us a room is just a room – a place with furniture providing an environment in which we live different aspects of our day-to-day lives. It can have a range of physical elements that dictate how we inhabit the space and we may find ourselves responding to whether the room is warm or cold, bright or dingy, functional or decorative and whether it makes us feel at ease or uncomfortable. We may take away a general impression of the room when we leave, but usually the room is incidental, little more than a backdrop to what happens in it.

Our experience at Trigonos suggests that if you ask people to describe the picture above a fireplace, the colour of the curtains or the texture of a chair cover once they have left a room, most of them will not be able to do so even if they have been in it many times and even if they are the person who regularly cleans it! But does that mean the décor of the room is unimportant?

Of course there is a difference between a conscious awareness of one's surroundings (as in being able to remember physical details) and a more unconscious awareness (when recalling the room triggers a more elusive, perhaps emotional, response). And, undoubtedly, some people have a high level of

Main meeting room

Small meeting room

sensitivity to indoor spaces and experience a room (or, as described in the quote below, a house) as having a spirit or soul as E.M. Forster suggests:

> *"To them Howards End was a house: they could not know that to her it had been a spirit…"*[22]

There are a number of components that combine to create the ambience of any internal space, including the room's size and shape; style of furniture; colour scheme; textures; temperature; lighting; views of the outside as well as the artefacts that adorn the walls or flat surfaces. Do the various components enhance each other or clash? What is experienced as harmonious and what is simply dull? When is a room exciting and challenging and when just ugly and brutal?

Much of this could be seen as a matter of taste and personal preference, but it may be more complex and interesting than that. For example, one may not like the ornate décor of Versailles yet still find it satisfying because it has a strong sense of coherence which may equally be the case in a simple shepherd's hut.

We are speaking here of indoor spaces that work because they have a subtle but tangible sense of 'emotional truth' or 'emotional substance' – an internal environment that speaks to the soul and brings with it a sense of containment, safety and quiet inspiration without imposing a point of view.

So far, we have considered rooms as a whole entity, but mention must be made of the artistic works that hang on many of the walls and that have a key role in giving each space both definition and personality. In this regard, the work of textile artist Eta Ingham Lawrie makes a remarkable contribution to Trigonos.

There are large pieces in many of the public spaces and smaller pieces hang in some of the bedrooms. What is it that makes them so special?

Each piece is unique, handcrafted, made from natural fibres and items from nature and in subtle but vibrant colours from natural dyes. They are the antithesis of the mass-produced images that we see on most walls in public spaces and, probably because her work conveys movement, light and warmth rather than illustration, it is open to individual experience and interpretation.

Eta's work has a tangible but unobtrusive presence. For example, in one of the meeting rooms (see page 63), the wall-hanging closely echoes the landscape through the window next to which it hangs and provides a visual, if subconscious, connection for those in the room between inside and outside whilst leaving the space free for them to pursue their activities.[23]

---

22   E.M. Forster, *Howards End,* 1910.

23   For more about Eta Ingham Lawrie's work see: *Light, Warmth & Life*, compiled by Ros Tennyson and published by Ruskin Mill Trust in collaboration with Trigonos in 2022.

Eta's hanging on the staircase at Plas

There are, of course, several other factors that influence our response to the internal environment, as well as what hangs on the walls. Rooms need to 'breathe' and to do this they need to be devoid of unnecessary clutter. In our own homes, a level of clutter works because the objects have history and meaning that we hold on to as an expression and reinforcement of who we are. However, in public spaces, clutter is intrusive and gets in the way. For a room to breathe, it needs a sense of spaciousness and a level of simplicity.

Perhaps an example is useful here: it took one of our regular volunteers to point out the difference when the bookshelves in the library were jammed full of books and when clusters of books were interspersed with different artefacts, drawing one's eye to the shelves because they were interesting rather than oppressive. You can judge for yourself the difference between the shelf on the left and the shelf on the right (see page 66).

There is also the issue of symmetry versus asymmetry and here we were on shaky ground since we learnt that, to certain members of the Trigonos team, symmetry was essential and asymmetry gave them considerable discomfort. Clearly our brains are wired quite differently in this regard and it can be (and was) challenging to find ways to bridge this divide. But as John Ruskin points out:

"No human face is exactly the same in its lines on each side, no leaf perfect in its lobes, no branch in its symmetry. All admit irregularity as they imply change; and to banish imperfection is to destroy expression, to check exertion, to paralyse vitality."[24]

As the decision-makers, our preference for the rationale behind Ruskin's asymmetry prevailed, but many a tense conversation was had with some of our colleagues in the hospitality team about why an asymmetrical approach to populating the mantelpiece in the library was preferable (see page 67).

---

24   John Ruskin, *Stones of Venice*, 1854.

Asymmetrical

Symmetrical

The last element in this necessarily brief exploration of the importance of décor is to do with paying attention to detail – whether this is the small vases of flowers in the bedrooms, the candles and colourful napkins on the dining room table at dinner or anticipating what might be needed to make each visitor comfortable.

As Trigonos evolved, we came to realise that décor was not incidental but mattered a great deal and was actually quite fundamental in its influence and impact on those who visited as well as those who worked there. Whilst the landscape is of great significance in drawing people into the *'genius loci'*[25], the internal setting is of real importance in embracing them with a sense of care, warmth and vitality.

---

25 The term *'genius loci'* originates in Roman mythology and refers to the protective spirit of a place.

> *Trigonos sits in a location with astonishing views and ever-changing moods.*
>
> *People have their individual ways of relating to this dramatic contrast, and it has always felt important to give our visitors the opportunity to experience it as deeply as possible.*
>
> *Our approach to working the land always tried to take account of its many purposes and to understand it as a setting for significant experience as well as its potential for productivity and environmental protection.*

Judy

Visitors

> "The experience of being at Trigonos is more than the sum of its parts, there is something extra. I think this is because the people who run the place do so because they believe in and care about what they do in a way that goes beyond a well-run business. Trigonos consistently gets rave reviews from the participants who come on our Mindfulness courses – in particular for the added element of a civilised and caring way of living in a world that often seems woefully short of such qualities."[26]

Our initial offer was focused on two areas: Firstly, courses where we would provide the course leader as well as the facilities. Secondly, advertising our facilities and services to groups who had their own programmes and needed no further engagement from us outside of our hospitality role.

The first paying group of guests came from Germany. They were a group of students studying medicine from an anthroposophical perspective who wanted a quiet retreat atmosphere for their time studying together. They stayed for several weeks and their great appreciation of the place was a huge endorsement at such a crucial early stage. Members of that group re-visited us about 15 years later when we were able to remember and celebrate our importance to them and their importance to us.

Soon a number of visiting groups were returning on a regular basis that helped to create a level of financial stability and confidence about the viability of Trigonos and its future prospects.

An ongoing arrangement evolved with the Centre for Mindfulness Research and Practice (CMRP) based at Bangor University. This was in the early days of the development of mindfulness practice in the UK and Trigonos became CRMP's main base for residential training courses in Wales. Over time the numbers of courses, mostly of a full week's duration and often with as many as 25 participants, grew to 18 a year at its height, meaning we had a reliable income stream as well as a deepening relationship with the fine group of course leaders. In addition, we benefited from the fact that many of the course participants returned to Trigonos on other courses or just for personal retreats because they enjoyed the place so much.

Trigonos was also the birthplace of what has now become a globally-recognised programme of work to train people to 'broker' partnerships between governments, business and non-profit organisations for sustainable and inclusive development (that threefold approach again). Over the years, this programme brought many people from across the world to Trigonos (someone from New Caledonia, an island in the Pacific Ocean, had a 36-hour journey!)

---

26   David Elias, trainer with the Centre for Mindfulness Research and Practice, Bangor University, c.2002.

Visitors in the studio

creating, for a few days, a mini United Nations in the small village of Nantlle.

So people came to Trigonos for many different purposes and from a range of contexts throughout and beyond the UK. Over the 24 years we were there, we never kept a tally of how many people came to Trigonos, or where they came from, or how many returned and how often. But to give an impression of the range and numbers involved, an analysis of the 73 groups that came in the year 2018–19 reveals that we had 1,265 individuals[27] who came on courses, workshops or retreats in the following categories:

- Arts
- Cooking
- Crafts
- Dance
- Education (schools and universities)
- International Development
- Mindfulness
- Outdoor Activities
- Professional Development
- Singing
- Spiritual Paths
- Tai Chi
- Yoga

---

27 The number of 'bed nights' (i.e. occupancy numbers) was 5,146 which means an average stay of four nights per person.

We also hosted our own courses in: Original Vision (Maria Hayes); Re-wilding the Mind (Jonathan Stacey and Claire Thomson); Space to Be (Ros Tennyson) and Weaving and Dyeing (Eta Ingham Lawrie) as well as occasional wedding celebrations and extended family events. And there were frequent impromptu celebrations!

That the hospitality team was appreciated by our visitors is shown by the feedback comments that came from one of the groups – these are typical of the feedback we received over the years:

- The staff were wonderful, the food exceptional, the setting and space very important
- Rooms were very comfortable and spotless
- Wonderful gardens with places to discover and explore
- Such care and kindness
- Great attention to detail
- The space to make this place home
- Beautiful wall hangings and flowers in the rooms
- The food – absolutely delicious
- Staff very unobtrusive but meeting all our needs
- The gracious way every request is met

Of course, the gifts and contributions were never just one-way, many times whilst taking a quiet walk through the wooded areas or down by the lake we found evidence of the visitors themselves enhancing the place, for example, this sculpture of stones.

Gate to walled garden

Walled garden

"Each new visitor was a fresh encounter giving us a real sense of pleasure as we watched them making the unfamiliar familiar each in their own way.

Wherever they came from and whether they had come for work, training or volunteering, the deeper value of Trigonos came from an almost invisible relationship between all of those things in a setting in which people felt they could truly be themselves."

Judy

Values

We did, in our many pre-Trigonos conversations, spend some time exploring our respective priorities, ideas and aspirations. These tended to align around the concept of 'three-some-ness'. As directors, we always carried our values and beliefs quite lightly but that does not mean that we had none or that they, however unarticulated, were not of considerable influence in everything we did. Retrospectively, we could summarise our core values as being to:

- Enable visitors to achieve all that they wanted during their stay while also giving them the space to discover things they had not anticipated
- Be transparent in our operations, provide good value for money and to keep charges at as modest a level as possible[28] while allowing for a surplus to be generated for further investment and development
- Provide all employees, volunteers and students with fair rewards, an enjoyable and safe working environment and the opportunity to develop their interests, capacities and ambitions. All waged and salaried people had a proper contract of employment that included meeting minimum wage legislation (and more) whilst never using zero hours contracts
- Work with (and perhaps influence) a range of local community groups in whatever ways were practical to maintain and improve the natural, built and social environments (e.g. being part of the Welsh government's *Communities First* programme), whilst supporting the principle of equity in financial dealings and economic development
- Ensure that the company could sustain its operations in the long-term while continuing to operate in line with its other stated values.

As mentioned above, 'Trigonos' means a three-sided figure – a triangle – a form that gains its strength and solidity from the presence of all three sides. Remove or disconnect one and the form collapses. In due course, we found a way of describing the complex and inter-dependent nature of what we were striving to achieve by using the triangle itself as an explanatory device and by trying to position our small effort in the far wider concept of 'three-folding' – as illustrated on page 76.

To maintain a perfect equilateral triangle in all circumstances is unrealistic, so the image of a triangle does have its limitations. An equilateral triangle means

---

28 Our hope was to minimise the risk of financial exclusion although, of course, even our modest charges were high for many who might have benefited. With events for which we were responsible, we introduced a bursary system open to any applicant.

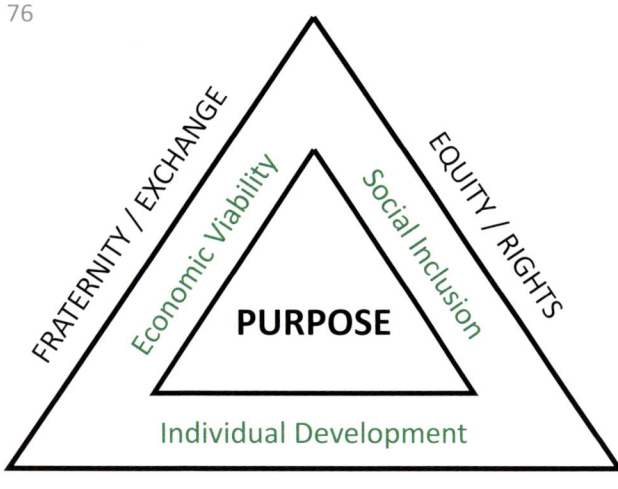

LIBERTY / VISION[29]

that each side is the same as the others – but this is a measurement of physical length only, rather than indicating equitable treatment. At any one time, we would find ourselves needing to be more focused on one aspect over another (on economic viability rather than individual development or vision, for example). But we always kept all three aspects in mind and sought to redress any imbalance that seemed to be occurring (for example, too much focus on economic viability and too little on social inclusion). We used the triangle as a way of holding each other to account for achieving a balance in what we were doing on a day-to-day basis.

In any case, the triangle may suggest a 'neatness' that is far from reality and the impact of one aspect on another could be quite complex and not allowing for simplistic 'value judgement'. To be true to ethical values when sourcing food, for example, we often eschewed the cheapest available produce even though this would reduce our gross profit margin that in turn could have negatively impacted our ethical commitment to a fair wage. But our values-driven approach to food became an important factor for those visitors choosing to come to Trigonos. So more visitors came, which in turn led to increased profits that enabled us to fulfil our commitment to paying our colleagues well.

To illustrate what we meant by the 'interdependence' at the heart of our (perhaps any) project, we can take another triangle:

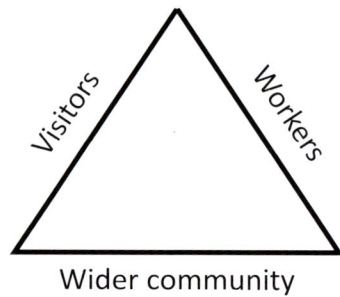

In this triangle, we capture the essentially interdependent nature of our key day-to-day relationships: **visitors** providing the income and the rationale that both ensures and justifies the organisation's survival, whilst **workers** are providing the visitors with what

---

29 The term 'vision' is used to mean 'imaginative and future thinking' rather than a more formal 'vision statement' which, as we have mentioned earlier, we never had.

they need and the **wider community** is providing the enabling environment which the organisation and the workers both need in order to thrive.

The clear inter-dependence between these groups is explicit and shows that it is to the advantage of all to co-operate in achieving both individual and shared goals rather than seeking to exploit each other to maximise their immediate (and possibly short-term) gains. However, this approach does have its limitations – whilst it may be clear that these three kinds of relationships are inter-connected, it does not tell us anything about the quality of those inter-connected relationships.

In reality, the triangles at Trigonos were never equilateral in terms of value given. Running a business is a constant challenge to bring the different elements as near to balance as possible – a constant juggling act. Our philosophy and values were there, and both influenced and guided us in the endless judgements to be made and the decisions we took.

> *Even after 22 years, people were still asking: What was your vision in the beginning? Did you have a mission? Have you achieved what you set out to do? These always remained questions.*
>
> *All I feel able to say with hindsight is that we followed opportunities as they arose whilst at the same time learning to be patient and wait rather than make rash decisions.*

Judy

Further Reflections

Reflections in the lake

Our social business approach

Having conveyed something of what we did and how we worked, it feels right to start this section on 'reflections' by considering our experience in creating and operating as a social business.

When we moved in, we found that everything had been left untouched since the closure of the Plas as an arts centre. It felt as if the building was holding its breath, waiting for something to happen, with condiments left on the dining room tables; laundry cupboards full of sheets and towels; furniture all in place; office papers and records sitting on shelves and in filing cabinets. With only one exception, there was very little that required urgent attention. The exception was the dining room ceiling that had been damaged by water from a burst pipe resulting from the previous very cold winter. Once this was repaired and re-decorated, and with a thorough cleaning of all rooms, we were indeed ready to open for business.

Cleaning and re-decorating were greatly helped by the arrival of large numbers of friends and relatives who came to stay with that purpose in mind. Some of them camped in the grounds and others occupied the bedrooms (prior to cleaning them!). As the dining room was out of use for several months, we cooked on two hotplates and gathered for communal meals in the large studio. In addition to giving their labour free of charge, those who could afford to also gave a contribution to cover the costs of their food and many also made generous donations to help us to cover running costs in the early months during that first winter when it was unlikely that we would have many paying guests.

At this time David Holgarth joined us as our first resident volunteer, having given up his secure job and his flat in London to do so. His input over five years was invaluable. David was an essential member of initial resident group, his ever-ready humour put a shine on all tasks and situations.

At the start, David, Judy and Richard effectively worked as full-time volunteers only in receipt of board and lodging. Ros, also worked on a volunteer basis part-time (when not working abroad), and Jean (who was retired), made her contribution by entertaining guests and keeping an eye on the library. Some 'pocket money' was paid as soon as paying guests arrived on a more regular basis, and this system continued in various forms for about five years as we worked to establish a sustainable business.

Between us, we covered all the work that had to be undertaken, including doing the cleaning, catering and running repairs as well as hosting those who came to stay. We all did a lot of washing up – only succumbing to a dishwasher, when we could afford it, and some five years after we started.

Jean Lynch, David Holgarth, Richard, Ros and Judy – Trigonos's founding residents (plus three children not pictured here!)

This was a form of *pro bono publico*[30] work. Whilst we retained the services of external professionals (builders, solicitors and bankers) by paying them the rate for the job, we relied heavily on pro bono contributions for most other tasks. This may have been a high-risk way to proceed, but we had little choice and it proved to be pivotal in evolving a sustainable business model that worked.

---

30 Which in the UK most commonly applies to the private sector where professionals, such as lawyers and bankers, offer their specialist skills at little or no charge, for the benefit of the community or NGOs, rather than for shareholder profit.

Even when we were earning enough to pay people, we offered salaries that were far from lavish both as a matter of social business principle and because anything else would have been unsustainable. We managed for many years to keep the pay differential between those we employed very small, though to attract people with the experience we needed to take over key management roles we did have to offer somewhat higher salaries in the last few years. Even then, the largest differential between the lowest and highest paid employee was only 35%.

As part of this financial picture, it is important to mention that both of the directors earning salaries (Judy and Richard) opted to work at a basic salary level – less than other senior colleagues – and the third (Ros), who was earning independently from external work, was able to work at Trigonos on a pro bono basis and to offer some additional contributions by paying for some modest capital expenses.

The point here is that, as founding directors, we were motivated by our commitment to 'living more lightly' so, for us, we chose only to earn what was necessary in favour of ensuring Trigonos was sustainable and that we could confidently employ others on long-term contracts.

As the business slowly grew we began to employ a few local people from Nantlle itself and the neighbouring villages of Talysarn and Penygroes.

We started with young people, mainly those who had just left school and for whom there were very limited local opportunities. We gave them letters of appointment that included a job description and their terms and conditions, as well as initial training and on-going support and supervision. Every team member working in the buildings also completed the Level 2 Food Safety and Hygiene course – for those with few or no GCSEs this was itself a milestone.

The workforce expanded to include people with more experience and specific skills, but also some who were coming back to work after having children or who had not been able to maintain employment except for short periods for one reason or another.

By 2016 we had a total of 20 full-time or part-time employees whose jobs were established and secure. As the numbers employed grew, so did our local reputation and it became increasingly easy to fill vacancies as they arose.

As one of the former staff said recently:

> "Working at Trigonos was like being part of a family much more than being just a member of the team. I haven't worked anywhere else where everyone sat down together and felt completely comfortable chatting – whether in English or Welsh – as we ate our lunch."

To paraphrase Schumacher: Trigonos was a business run as if people mattered.[31]

Over time we built a small management team to share responsibility for carrying out the day-to-day running of the project, whether in administration, land work, catering, cleaning or hosting. Many of those on the management team were internal promotions offering opportunities to individuals showing promise. Several stayed for many years and, when they eventually moved on, others came because they had heard it was a good place to work.

Once we had set up Trigonos as a company, we approached a firm of accountants to ask them to manage the preparing of the end-of-year accounts and making the annual returns to Companies House and HMRC. When we told them that we were not to be the owners of the company but using a company limited by guarantee, they strongly advised us not to do so but to retain the ownership to ourselves and then let the property to Trigonos as our trading company. We rejected that advice for the reasons given elsewhere.

Later, when our turnover was getting very near to the limit that normally required VAT registration, the same accountants advised us to register for VAT, which we duly did. For some reason we then carried out our

---

[31] *Small is Beautiful: A Study of Economics as if People Mattered,* by Fritz Schumacher, 1973.

own assessment of the VAT implications of our work and discovered that the rules at the time meant that we, as an educational services provider, did not in fact need to register for VAT. This was a pretty major error by our accountants that proved expensive for us. We then decided to change accountants and appointed John Hart who'd been the accountant to the Peter Bedford Trust (see page 22) and had a warm commitment to our project.

So we de-registered from VAT. But a few years later the government changed the VAT rules, as a result of which only self-generated educational events (not those that were simply hosted by an educational services provider) qualified for VAT exemption. So we had to re-register and pay VAT on the largest part of our turnover.

That experience was a classic example of how we had to learn from our (or others') mistakes and to cope with an ever-changing business environment that was almost entirely outside our control. In the above case we had to work hard in making arrangements to manage the resulting increased costs. In fact, the VAT change had a greater impact on us than the economic crisis created by the banking collapse of 2008.

Alongside this, it was critically important to get ourselves known. So early on we created our first publicity leaflets and notepaper. We used our name, the image of our triskele and a strapline: *Learning • Discovery • Retreat* to give the project a strong identity. 'Learning' and 'Retreat' were references to our purpose, as outlined in our company objectives and were the basis of what drew people to visit us. 'Discovery' was an added invitation to explore what might be encountered simply by being in such a special place with its vibrant spirit and ever-changing weather.

After a few years we were a modestly successful social business – but as all small business people know, it is never possible to take your eye off the ball and unexpected external events can hit you hard: for instance, the change in VAT regulation, the economic crisis of 2008 and, more recently, the arrival of the Covid 19 pandemic.

As the business grew it became necessary to provide more accommodation for guests. This was achieved by all the founding residents and the three children moving into housing in the village, which released eight more rooms for the benefit of visitors. This meant that there was no longer a Trigonos team member living on the site which, at the time, felt like quite a risk, since our overnight presence allowed for there to be constant cover. But the downside to this was that some guests did not appreciate that we (and our children) also needed 'down time' and expected 24-hour attention. When we moved into accommodation in the village we devised an on-call system to enable us to respond to any overnight difficulties. It was rare that we were called out overnight, though insects did have a nasty habit of setting off the fire alarms.

To bring further structure to how we operated as a social business, we created written policies covering key areas including:
- Sustainability
- Equal opportunities
- Language
- Food

We wanted these policies to be appropriate for our particular circumstances and values rather than 'off the shelf' versions. We give one example – our food policy – to illustrate our approach to policy-making:

> **Trigonos food policy**
> We believe food – how it is sourced, prepared and served – is very important and it is clear that this is also seen by many of our guests as a key feature of our offer and is highly valued. Our aim is to provide wholesome, freshly prepared, locally sourced (where possible) and nourishing vegetarian dishes that satisfy the tastes and appetites of all who come, whether or not they are vegetarian. For those guests who are not vegetarian, we seek to introduce vegetarian cuisine by offering an inspiring vegetarian experience rather than by proselytising.

Trigonos was registered with the Wholesome Food Association and we aligned ourselves wholeheartedly with their definition:

> *"Wholesome food is grown and processed using sustainable, non-polluting methods as close as possible to those found in nature. Wholesome food is, wherever possible, traded and consumed within a short distance of where it was grown. Wholesome food is an integral part of life and community, rather than merely a commodity for profit."*[32]

In terms of sustainability, we aspired to becoming 'zero-waste' in our catering – which meant moving on surplus food to those who needed it, recycling food waste and reducing our use of non-recyclable plastic and other non-recyclable packaging. This was not a 'quick fix' and we always knew it would take time and a concerted effort to achieve.

If all this sounds too ideal to be true, we should also clarify that not everything was plain sailing. Perhaps four things are worth mentioning in this regard:

First, we never really 'cracked' the challenge of marketing and communications,[33] so while creating our own suite of courses was relatively easy, getting a

---

32 https://www.wholesome-food.org/
33 This improved markedly when younger members of the administrative team brought their social media skills to address the challenge.

satisfactory up-take proved to be very difficult. Whilst the weaving courses run several times a year by Eta Ingham Lawrie were often over-subscribed, others, with equally skilled and experienced trainers or facilitators, all too often had to be cancelled through lack of bookings, especially in the early days. Some of the early choices we made about courses were misguided, focusing too much on matters covered by others elsewhere without much relevance to our specific location and approach.

Second, we never earned enough surplus income to invest as fully as we wanted to in the development of our land work. We needed a barn and more modern equipment to reach scale and efficiencies that are particularly hard to achieve when working organically. We made several grant applications to support these developments, but without success, though we did get a grant from Environment Wales to plant 2,000 trees and replenish hedges and then a further grant to fund a land manager at a modest salary for three years.

Third was the fact that the responsibility we carried for co-leading a complex project of this kind, whilst both satisfying and exhilarating, was often exhausting because it was a complex and ambitious project and there was always so much to be done.

This may be a factor in the fourth challenge — which was the issue of handing over. It proved to be extremely hard to encourage those who became team leaders and proved themselves to be highly competent, committed and reliable, to step up into a director-level role. This became a central issue when it came to 'succession planning' and meant we had to think more creatively about who and what would follow on from us.

"Visiting Trigonos — experiencing the idea, the place and most importantly, its people — felt like taking an essential breath in our increasingly hectic world. It offered an important lesson to those seeking inspiration in how to live and work more purposefully in the world."

Julie Mundy (from Australia),
Trigonos visitor and attendee, 2014–2018

The key purpose of Trigonos as a social business is the provision of hospitality to as wide a range of people and groups as possible, with a strong orientation towards educational groups.

When we opened for business we didn't have a document that described how we wanted to operate as a provider of hospitality — we didn't really think of ourselves in this way — this was something that only became obvious and more conscious over time.

Richard

Hospitality

It took us some years to recognise that we were in the business of hospitality! Perhaps this was because of the term is so often used in terms of being a 'sector' or, even worse, an 'industry'. We simply didn't see what we were offering in those ways. We had quite a different perspective and were heartened to come across a book of essays, relatively recently, by the Nigerian author, Ben Okri[34] who opens his eloquent piece on hospitality with the idea that: *Hospitality begins in the soul.*

He goes on to say:

"Hospitality is more than a rational, deliberate act. It is a way of being. The idea of hospitality is challenged most when we are dealing with the unknown. It means that we have faith first even before we have evidence."

This, coupled with our day-to-day experiences of acting as hosts, made us think more consciously about the nature and history of hospitality. As indicated in the work of O'Gorman (a researcher in the field of hospitality and tourism),[35] hospitality is central to all human societies and can be regarded as a fundamental mark of civilisation. Another academic, O'Connor says hospitality has, from the earliest time been key to human relationships:

"In societies as far apart as the New Guinea Highlands and the Amazon rainforest feasting, and the hospitality that this signifies, consolidates and / or establishes links between groups of kin, and is an integral part of the process of drawing and redrawing the parameters of alliances between such groups."[36]

In O'Connor's view, only once an understanding of hospitality's origins and its place in human nature is achieved can we expect to understand what hospitality could truly mean today.

Hospitality is a key feature in many Western and Middle-Eastern religious teachings as in:

"... the Judaeo-Christian traditions, where the outsider's status is changed from stranger to guest and where the guest is under the protection of the host. With that hospitality comes a responsibility from the guest to the individual householder. In ancient Greece, hospitality tended to move from domestic provision to the public domain. Then in classical Roman times commercial hospitality was created to provide for people who did not have access to private/ domestic hospitality."[37]

---

34 'Hospitality', from a collection of essays entitled: *A Time for New Dreams* by Ben Okri, 2011.
35 *The Origins of Hospitality and Tourism* by Kevin O'Gorman, Goodfellow Publishers Ltd, 2010.
36 'Towards a new interpretation of "hospitality"' by Daniel O'Connor from *The International Journal of Contemporary Hospitality Management,* Volume 17, Number 3.
37 O'Gorman, Ibid.

This breadth of approach is illustrated in the story of Abraham/Ibrahim which is found in the Torah, the book of Genesis (where it is called 'Abraham and Sarah's Hospitality') and in the Qar'an. *The Old Trinity* by Andrei Rublev (see page 91) – a 15th-century Russian icon painter – illustrates the story of three people visiting Abraham/Ibrahim and Sarah at the oak of Mamre. They do not recognise the visitors as angels, but rather see them simply as weary travellers in need of hospitality, which they willingly provide.

This picture is often cited as a rendition of the spirit of hospitality, and it is surely no coincidence that Ros came across a batik copy of the painting in a Moscow flea-market many years before she came to Wales, and when we moved in she hung it above the fireplace in the Trigonos library without knowing that this picture was associated with the theme of hospitality.

To complete this brief overview of the origins and nature of hospitality in those societies that have a written history, we should also consider how it manifests in China where it is underpinned by the traditions of Daoism, Buddhism and Confucianism:

> *"The Daoist philosophy of hospitality is a 'trying not to try' (a state of wu-wei), in which we refrain from representing, classifying or naming the stranger, and welcome him in wu-wei, revealing the ultimate oneness of the Dao. Unconditional hospitality is hospitality in its purest form, but in its purest form it is also the least attainable, because it embodies both hospitality and its opposite (hostility). Chinese Buddhism also embraces the concept of unconditional hospitality in which the host recognizes himself in the other and thereby recognizes the interdependency of everything.*
>
> *For Confucianism, this life is about doing the right thing in any given situation. Recognizing what is the right thing to do for Confucius is a matter of training and experience. Only the virtuous man who has trained himself extensively recognizes what is needed in a particular situation."*[38]

In this description we see the potential conflict between hospitality as an innate and positive human characteristic, and hospitality that must be worked at and even imposed by rules, perhaps more akin to the modern 'hospitality industry' where hospitality now most commonly refers to the vast businesses connected to global tourism.

---

[38] *An Asian Ethics of Hospitality: Hospitality in Confucian, Daoist and Buddhist philosophy*, Martine Berenpas, Leiden University, Institute for Philosophy, 2016.

Old Trinity by Andrei Rublev, now hanging in the Trinity Lavra of St Sergius in Sergiyev Posad, Russia

But we find something reassuringly different in Rory Stewart's account of his journey on foot from Iran through Afghanistan to Nepal in 2002. He says his progress, indeed his very survival, was made possible because of the unsolicited help of local people. He paints an extraordinary and moving picture of how he was assisted on his way. Of the many people he met, he says that:

> "... they were not all saints, though some of them were. A number were greedy, idle, stupid, hypocritical, insensitive, mendacious, ignorant and cruel. Some of them had robbed or killed others and many of them threatened me and begged from me. But never in my 21 months of travel did they attempt to kidnap or kill me. I was alone and the stranger, walking in very remote areas; I represented a culture that many of them hated and I was carrying enough money to save or at least transform their lives. In more than 500 village houses, I was indulged, fed, nursed and protected by people poorer, hungrier, sicker and more vulnerable than myself."[39]

Stewart saw the connection between hospitality and its opposite (hostility). During his long journey, those he met included Sunni and Shia Muslims in Iran and Afghanistan; Christians in Pakistan; Sikhs, Brahmins and Dalits in India, and Buddhists in Nepal, who gave him hospitality without any expectation of reward. In conclusion he states: "*I owe this journey and my life to them.*"

A final reflection on the role of hospitality, and its central part in our social business, comes from Daniel O'Connor who raises a point we often considered at Trigonos, in observing:

> "The idea that in every human there exists to varying degrees a natural level of hospitableness, becomes more believable the more it is pondered. The word natural can be defined as being born with a particular skill or quality. Therefore it is reasonable to assume that genuine hospitableness cannot be developed or grown over time but is instead printed onto our character or personality at birth, almost genetically."[40]

How does this align (or not) with our experiences with Trigonos?

O'Connor's statement reflects, in part, what we learnt from engaging local people to work at Trigonos: that there is something deeply rooted in people's innate capacities to be hospitable. But our experience is at odds with his statement that hospitality "cannot be developed or grown over time", since we watched individual members of the team grow increasingly sociable, warm and welcoming without ever being 'trained' in hospitality

---

39   *The Places In Between,* Rory Stewart, Picador, 2014.

40   Daniel O'Connor, Ibid.

skills or even being asked to 'be hospitable'. Once this capacity was released, it became central to the experience of those visiting Trigonos and was commonly mentioned in feedback.

What does it take to achieve this? Ben Okri answers this question well:

> "Hospitality is not tolerance or charity, nor is it weakness. Hospitality can only come from true strength of knowing what one is, and the tranquillity of allowing other people the strength of what they are."[41]

Those who worked at Trigonos did not have to know about those who came our way as our guests – they simply needed to be open, welcoming and tolerant of what made some of our visitors different.

Okri takes his view of hospitality one stage further and we particularly appreciated his notion of 'invisible hospitality' – that which is given intuitively by those who offer it and is experienced unconsciously by those who receive it.

> "There is also intellectual hospitality, the hospitality to ideas, to dreams, to ways of seeing, to perception, to cultures. We will call this invisible hospitality. This is the most important hospitality of all and includes all of the hospitalities."[42]

We think that many guests (or their group leaders) who came to Trigonos did so because they had an instinct for what we could offer. It is perhaps not surprising that we were rarely faced with decisions about whether or not to say 'no' to an enquiry from a group leader. There may well have been many types of group or guest that we would not have been comfortable entertaining, but only once in 24 years did we say 'no' to a potential group and this was on the basis that their self-described programme would be likely to cause discomfort to our staff and potentially have a negative impact on the local community, which could have done lasting damage to our key local relationships.

As for our position on the spectrum of what constitutes hospitality, a linking theme emerges – the persistence of the virtues of friendship. This runs through the work of Ivan Illich (another inspirational figure) who, in a conversation with Jerry Brown (the ex-governor of California) on his radio show,[43] observed: that in classical society, hospitality was 'a condition consequent on a good society in politics' but that he now believed that: 'hospitality might be the starting point of politics.'

---

41   Ben Okri, Ibid.
42   Ibid.

43   *We the People* KPFA – (uncorrected manuscript) March 22, 1996.

He goes on to conclude:

> "… if I had to choose one word to which hope can be tied, it is hospitality. A practice of hospitality and generating seedbeds for virtue and friendship on the one hand and on the other hand… radiating out for rebirth of community."

Trigonos, as it evolved, did not conform to the modern understanding of commercial hospitality, but neither was it an example of unconditional hospitality as credited to Chinese Buddhism. Rather it was an endeavour that ranged across many conceptions of hospitality without belonging to a single interpretation of the term. We felt Trigonos had become a place where hospitality supported: unexpected connections being made; friendships created or deepened, and the seeding of ideas about what it means to belong in ways that might be of benefit to the wider world.

> "The Trigonos story is about the emergence of an increasingly pragmatic, purposeful and self-aware hospitality-as-transformation. It may not have been the initial intention but, over the years, it is this that has been of real benefit to all those it has touched in ways both intended and unintended."[44]

Sundial in the evening

---

44   Rafał Serafin, Associate, Partnership Brokers Association.

'The setting of Trigonos is so stunning it served to constantly remind us that we were 'stewards' not 'controllers' of the situation. We could not make Trigonos 'work', we could only do our best to enable it to develop.

Looking back over the years, the development process was much more about active waiting than active planning and also in coming to recognise how important the way we worked together was in supporting that approach.'

Ros

Shared leadership

From the day we moved in, the low-key way we worked together set the tone for the next 24 years. In the first hours following our arrival, without saying more than a couple of words to each other, we just naturally gravitated to our individual priorities and personal comfort zones. It was a way of settling our nerves whilst also, almost subconsciously, making a personal gesture to mark the moment in our individual ways.

Judy planted a tiny African violet just inside the gate of the overgrown walled garden and then went on to attack the waist-high brambles. Richard found a long ladder and started cleaning leaves, twigs and other accumulated debris from the gutters of the Plas. Ros hung pictures – including placing the batik of Rublev's *The Old Trinity* (illustrated on pages 67 and 91) above the fireplace in the room that would become the library and would, in due course, come to be seen as the place at the heart of our project.

So started, what we now realise, was a rather unique working relationship, though we didn't think of it as anything special at the time, that underpinned everything that followed. It is quite unusual for a project of this scale to be run by a triumvirate, especially one that remains unchanged for more than two decades. In fact, we were told repeatedly that 'triumvirates never work' but, although we never set out with the intention to do so, we proved the sceptics wrong.

In those early days we shared all the core jobs. For example, not being able to afford a professional chef, we took on the responsibility for cooking meals for the guests as well as for our families, sometimes cooking for as many as 40 people. Judy, a naturally talented cook, set a high standard that was inspiring as well as a little daunting.

There is something else in addition to our specific talents and experiences, which is more to do with our natures. Judy and Richard shared a more 'reflective' temperament that meant they were inclined to be thoughtful and considered in the way they worked and in making careful decisions. Ros, being more 'decisive' in temperament meant she was a quick thinker and made almost instant decisions that sometimes enabled us to collectively take bolder, if potentially riskier, steps. As it turned out, these characteristics complemented each other well, since Richard and Judy were happy when brave decisions were actually made over which they may have 'mulled' for some time, and Ros had no problem with being told every so often to 'slow down'.

This all took place within the context where each of us had our areas of full responsibility but needed joint agreement on over-lapping or especially important issues.

We all came to recognise that it was useful that Ros was often away from Trigonos with her international partnership work – this gave breathing space to the other two and it meant that Judy, who had never before had a leadership role in an organisation, was able to grow into the role over time. It became a wonderfully balanced relationship as we came to deeply know and respect each other's particular way of thinking and acting – relishing and building on the differences even when they could sometimes be irksome.

A sense of humour helped!

Over time, we intuitively found ways of working around specific things that could have undermined our tri-partite relationship (for example, sensitive issues to do with our children when we were all living on site) – not so much a case of avoiding the issue but rather letting it work itself out over time instead of risking the damage that would arise by taking a too fixed or challenging position.

Whilst we didn't focus over-much on the nature of our working relationship, we did entirely share the notion that we were operating as an act of service and that we were keen to provide an alternative to the dominance of a notion of leadership as a hierarchy of authority. The term 'shared leadership' describes it well, since we participated in all day-to-day operations as equals.

Another issue that is important to mention is the level of commitment we made as the project's founders. This is quite subtle and, therefore, difficult to convey. We all thought nothing, especially in the early days, of working far more than the 40 hours of a conventional working week when it was necessary. This does not mean that we never had time for ourselves, but such time was taken when it was possible, not as a matter of 'right'.

As surprising as it may seem to others, despite being the project's founders and directors, none of us felt possessive about it. We were delighted when it worked well without one or other of us, and we all developed a natural aptitude for stepping up and stepping back as seemed appropriate. This included, of course, stepping away completely when we handed the project over.

We ran Trigonos as its officially registered 'board of directors' – which sounds quite grand for a working relationship that was essentially based on friendship. It is undoubtedly true that the way Trigonos evolved owed much to the nature of our relationship – and as Judy observed:

> *"We three people, with our very different personalities, experiences and capacities, had to build from what we knew and find a way of working for a common purpose in order to do something useful."*

Perhaps the two most important lessons here are: don't be put off by anyone telling you that something 'never works', and recognise the fact that building initiatives around people is far more productive, engaging and sustainable, than building people around projects.

"The wellspring of trust that existed between us never had an explicit purpose, but it allowed us to make decisions, to take the necessary risks and to find ways through all manner of difficulties, personal, financial and material.

*It always felt that we were guardians of something important even if we couldn't quite define it.
I often wonder where that came from."*

Judy

Lessons for others

So what more can we deduce from our 24 years setting up and running a social business and what might there be that could have value for others? As a company limited by guarantee, Trigonos had no shareholders, meaning that no individuals or group owned the company or its assets. This had important consequences – namely that we were:

- Able to fully focus on societal and environmental benefits, with any surplus income over expenditure enabling further investment and development, because maximising profits was never the objective of the company (as it is in most shareholder-owned companies)
- Free to ensure that a continuing contribution to the revitalisation of the environment and to providing value for the local community was paramount, since we could not sell the company or its assets for personal financial gain
- Able to operate independently within the parameters and values we chose that we felt were important, since Trigonos was neither a conventional business (so was without shareholders) nor a charity (so we did not have external trustees who may have inhibited our ideas or ways of working).

These are basic but important facts about the tangible benefits of being a social business and they cannot, in our view, be over-estimated.

What made it work so well? And what can we share that will encourage others to consider adopting a social business model for their own endeavours? There are a number of things that stand out.

We always tried to keep on our toes – being willing to let go of some plans for a while, when to pursue them would have been unrealistic and when others things became more important. This meant we were constantly juggling priorities, for example:

- Flood defences vs. agricultural barn
- Turning the shabbier bedrooms into en-suites vs. replacing the increasingly unreliable cooker and other basic equipment
- Offering an 'open door' policy for community activities vs. protecting the space for those wanting quiet retreats

As directors, we had to exercise judgment and take essential decisions continuously whilst doing our best not to default to a 'decision-by-committee' way of operating. We did this in the following ways:

- **Calling directors' meetings only when necessary** – (and often in the evenings over a glass of wine) avoiding the tendency to have meetings as a habit
- **Each of us being free to take unilateral decisions in our areas of expertise** – specifically where we were the designated lead (Richard on day-to-day management and financial management; Judy on the land and kitchen; Ros on décor and team-building) and only needing to agree a decision collectively when it had significant policy or financial implications
- **Not making major decisions until we all agreed** – it was vital that we all felt equally comfortable that it was the right decision to make
- **Constantly striving to find a balance** – especially in weighing attention to detail against 'bigger picture' thinking
- **Being prepared to say 'no'** – when we felt it was necessary and even if saying no made us appear difficult or even obstinate
- **Keeping meticulous records of all our meetings** – the more unorthodox our approach, the more we knew we had to be rigorous in meeting external expectations in terms of our annual financial and company reports, tax returns, legal compliance, health and safety issues

And, above all, recognising that:

- **First and foremost Trigonos had to be a functional and sustainable business** – which meant that sometimes sound business and financial decisions had to take precedence over our more aspirational and speculative visions and ideas

We also had developed an instinct for seeing potential – for example, where some found the ever-present grey slate rather depressing: we were constantly surprised by its unexpected beauty.

Then came the whole issue of succession planning! Who or what would follow us?

We started thinking about this as early as 2010 and actually dedicated a couple of days to considering different succession scenarios which we now look back on with amusement since none of them were what actually happened. The options included:

- Growing a new trio of directors from within our existing team – or, failing that, more intentionally appointing people with the potential for becoming directors over time
- Handing over to our children – two of whom had expressed an interest in carrying on the work – when they had built enough experience to take on the project
- Selling the site at a modest price (essentially just enough to cover outstanding loans and other financial obligations) to a like-minded organisation that would commit to our social and environmental objectives

Or, as a last resort:

- Selling the site (which was valued at over £1,200,000 in 2018) to the highest – probably commercial – bidder and gifting the surplus funds to like-minded projects elsewhere.[45]

We kept these options in mind during the following years, though we all hoped that the first option (growing the future from within the team) would be the way forward as this seemed to be the most likely way for there to be continuity with what we had started. In the event, despite building a really gifted management team, it became clear that none of them wanted to take on the additional responsibility of being directors.

By 2019 the situation had become somewhat urgent as we were getting older (our average age was now 75) and both Judy and Richard had significant health issues that meant that they had to step back from their active roles in running the project, with Judy also having to resign as a director. This left Ros as the sole 'executive' director with Richard, and three newcomers as 'non-executive' directors.

This was not the end of our friendship but was, effectively, the end of our managing triumvirate and the start of something new.

The new regime worked well and the business continued to flourish – so much so that it was able to survive when Covid struck in March 2020. Trigonos was eligible for furlough payments for all staff during a protracted period of closure, which, together with two grants awarded by the Welsh government due to our small business and hospitality sector status, plus a low-interest loan from the Co-op Bank, meant that we still had a going concern at the time we gifted the company

---

45   Our constitution allowed for a commercial sale so long as we as individuals did not benefit financially – in other words, the money would have had to be reinvested in comparable not-for-profit projects.

and the site to the Ruskin Mill Trust[46] in September 2020.

We believe the Trust will both respect and grow the initiative and will add considerably to our endeavours in many ways, for example by:

- Having the resources to invest in developments we could never quite afford – for example, in making the land truly bio-dynamic
- Adding an additional dimension, with Trigonos becoming a place offering training and apprenticeships for young adults with complex needs
- Ensuring the site and the programme of work continue to contribute to the social, environmental and economic health of the Nantlle Valley in perpetuity by placing it in a Land Trust.[47]

Between 1996 and 2020, Trigonos had undoubtedly provided an opportunity to many for looking both inwards and outwards. It has been valued as a space simply to be, rather than to be something specific. This was an observation often made by group leaders whose participants seemed to find it very easy to make the place their own during their stay.

Has Trigonos been a model for others and / or could it be in the future?

Never a place for a closed group operating in isolation from the world's challenges, we tried to make somewhere in which it was possible to acknowledge these challenges and build the energy, imagination and confidence to help make things better. Several of those who came (some from as far away as Kenya, Cambodia and Brazil) have let us know that their stay at Trigonos inspired them to try something similar, building on their own cultures and contexts. This feels good – knowing that our efforts have given others confidence to find their own path rather than simply trying to adopt or copy what they have seen.

Above all, it is worth reminding readers that our average age was 50 when we embarked on the project, so it seems that age is not, of itself, an impediment to creative thinking and bold action! We hope that others will feel inspired to put their own social business initiatives into practice – to paraphrase Goethe (see quote on page 10):

> Whatever you do, or think you can do,
> just do it, do it now!

---

46   For more information about the extraordinary work of the Trust, see: https://rmt.org/
47   A community land trust is a not-for-profit organisation that holds land on behalf of a place-based community, whilst serving as the long-term steward for affordable housing, community gardens, civic buildings, commercial spaces and other community assets on behalf of a community.

Epilogue

An epilogue is often concerned with the issue of legacy. What endures when things change and move on? As we prepared to hand Trigonos over to the stewardship of others, this question was very real for us. In negotiating the transfer, how much could we insist on certain obligations being agreed in order to maintain the things we thought were important? Did we trust others to safeguard our values and not to simply transform all our hard work into something that might quickly become completely unrecognisable? Or, having made our decision to make the gift, should we simply let go, walk away and leave things to unfold however they might?

In the event, letting go was not as difficult as others had assumed we would find it. Some of our long-term team members found it harder than we did, but then they were remaining and were living daily with what was now missing. However, even that didn't last long – some left, others arrived and there was excitement about the new investments being made and the expanded direction of travel.

It seems to be the case that because none of the three of us was possessive by nature, and because we had always seen our relationship to Trigonos as that of 'guardians' rather than 'owners', moving on was simply part of the cycle of life rather than an ending. Perhaps we learnt this from Judy – whose profound connection to nature entered into our collective psyche.

Whilst we were in the final stages of putting this publication together, sadly, Judy died after some years living first with Parkinson's disease, then cripplingly painful arthritis and finally cancer. Those who knew her during this time will remember the astonishing fact that she kept gardening till nearly the end – mostly in her beloved walled garden – as well as actively supporting the energetic development of biodynamic agriculture in the fields and polytunnels which had become possible with the handover to Ruskin Mill Trust. For Judy, this was the culmination of her decades of commitment to revitalising the land in harmony with the seasons, weather and the influence of the planets.

For many years, until his death in February 2013, Judy worked on the land alongside her partner, Peter, and we are pretty confident that this is how she would like her contribution to Trigonos to be remembered.

Epilogue

Peter and Judy in the polytunnel

As Judy said, at the time of Peter's death:

"Working together for so many years and against many odds – not least the obstinately stony fields – formed the basis of our life together in the Nantlle Valley and I will always be grateful for the incredible opportunity that Trigonos brought with it and for having a companion who so deeply shared my commitment to the land."

The most fitting way we can draw this piece to a close is to suggest that relationships – like Judy and Peter's and like ours as the 'Trigonos triumvirate' – that are based on making the most of an incredible opportunity and a sense of shared purpose have a value and an impact that outlasts the little lives of the individuals involved.

Acknowledgements

Trigonos benefited from formal arrangements with three organisations providing students and adult volunteers on a regular basis:

Horizon International – providing students of 17–20 years of age for up to six weeks at a time and coming from Germany. For each one it was a huge learning curve – people, food, language, environment and work – everything was unfamiliar in this relatively remote place with limited social and cultural life and, until relatively recently, no mobile phone signal!

WWOOFers (an international organisation entitled Worldwide Working on Organic Farms). Over the years, some came with experience of organic horticulture, some had good land work knowledge and skills whilst others needed to be introduced to their first weed! Many had made use of this wonderful organisation to travel around the world offering their labour in return for board and lodging.

Drive for Youth bringing youngsters who were school refusers, disaffected or in trouble for one reason or another and who used their energy and muscle power to remarkable effect whether it was in digging brambles, getting rid of the dock plants in the fields, constructing slate fences or building raised vegetable and flowerbeds.

Over the years we had many people working with us all of whom deserve recognition and thanks but if we named everyone, what a long list this would be! But mention must be made of at least some – so here goes:

Abi (famous for her celebration cakes) • Adie (whose untimely death was a shock felt by all) • Alex (who could turn his hand to anything) • Amy (Terri-Anne's sister) • Andrew (an early land worker, originally from Holland) • Branwen (administrator for a stellar 10 years) • Claire (balancing work with being a single mum) • Cliff (purportedly 'retired' who worked as a volunteer on the land for 10 years) • Dafydd (started as a washer-up, then became our computer wizard) • Dave (the gentle giant) • David (the quiet gardener who helped Judy with the heavier work in the walled garden) • Ed (whose 'Trigonos Nut Roast' lives on) • Emma (Claire's sister and another whose tragic early death left everyone stunned) • Enfys (promoted to administrator from the hospitality team) • Frances (first administrator who set up the systems) • Geoffrey (who could talk

Acknowledgements

about prime numbers, advanced mathematics and higher spiritual beings in the same conversation) • Holger (the meteorologist from East Germany was promoted from cleaner to finance worker) • Iona (whose 'secret' fag breaks were notorious) • Jane (Abi's mum, persuaded to return to work by her daughter) • Jean ('the enchantress' who was one of the founding residents) • June (whose Welsh tea bread was eagerly awaited every Christmas) • Kayleigh (started with the washing up at 16 and returned 10 years later as Hospitality Manager) • Kieran (handy man extraordinaire) • Lee (author of *Peace and Parsnips*) • Lowri (project/finance manager and part-time poet) • Mandy (chef whose meals were a feast for the eyes as well as the stomach) • Mark (the skate-boarding, foraging chef) • Matt (Assistant chef, now General Manager!) • Mathew (Judy's talented carpenter/builder son) • Nikki (anything from baking to cooking to gardening to hosting) • Owain (sometimes with his two tri-lingual young sons in tow) • Rachel (combining evening work at Trigonos with her role as a teaching assistant in the local school) • Red (pioneered the role of hospitality manager) • Ricky (who helped washing up from the age of 13 and later returned to mend visitors' cars) • Sheila (who, to her surprise, was promoted from cleaner to team leader) • Sue (library organiser) • Terri-Ann (a model for us all with her equanimity and flexibility) • Val (highly competent stand-in chef, gardener and photographer).

Financial support in the form of gifts or no-interest loans were gratefully received from: Chris Freudenberg, Richard Grover, Philip Martyn, Rick Moxon, Mark Pickworth, Margot Tennyson, Ros Tennyson, Vivienne Wilkinson and others. Three legacies – from Margaret Duberley, Rosie Grover and Jean Lynch – helped us to get started and, later, to fund larger projects.

Last but not least, there are three people to whom we would like to express our gratitude for their role in becoming non-executive directors/board members of Trigonos in the last 18 months before we handed the project over in September 2020. Their rich and varied experiences, together with their warm enthusiasm for securing the future of Trigonos, were invaluable.

Jim Embrey – brought his many years' experience in tourism development, combined with his success in raising significant funds, to create a community project in his village.

Paul Garnault – brought his existing relationship to Ruskin Mill Trust and was ideally placed to help us in navigating the handover and then acting as a bridge between the old and the new.

Surinder Hundal – brought extensive commercial and communication experience with her that were very helpful, as was her skill in chairing the board through uncharted territory.

REFERENCES

Berenpas, M. – *An Asian Ethics of Hospitality: Hospitality in Confucian, Daoist and Buddhist Philosophy*, 2016, Leiden University, Institute for Philosophy.

Borrow, G. – *Wild Wales*, 1862.

Cohen, W. – Lessons from Peter Drucker, www.corporatelearningnetwork.com/column/lessons-from-drucker-cohen

Grover, R. – 'Another Path in Community Care', *The Friend*, June 26, 1992.

Grover, R., Harris, J., Tennyson, R. – 'Trigonos', *New View* magazine, Autumn 1999.

Illich, I. – 'We the People', KPFA (uncorrected manuscript) March 22, 1996.

Jones, G.P. – *The Heritage of Slate in the Nantlle Valley*, Trigonos.

Lao Tsu – *Tao Te Ching*, translators Gisa-Fu Feng and Jane English, Wildwood House, 1973.

Murray, W.H. – *The Evidence of Things Not Seen*, Baton Wicks, 2002.

O'Connor, D. – 'Towards a New Interpretation of "Hospitality"', *The International Journal of Contemporary Hospitality Management*, Volume 17, Number 3, 2005.

O'Gorman, K.D. – *The Origins of Hospitality and Tourism*, Goodfellow Publishers Ltd, 2010.

Peter Bedford Trust – *Free of Old Tags*, PBT 1968–1985, ISBN 0 948084 01 4.

Sorensen, M. – *Working on Self-Respect – Writings on Offenders and Other Homeless People*, PBT, 1986.

The Mabinogion – translated by Gwyn Jones and Thomas Jones, Everyman's Library, 2001.

For us as trainers and for our many participants, Trigonos provided a living example of what happens when there is clarity of intention, combined with deep care and attentiveness.

This powerful story of the creation and development of a social business offers vital pointers for how to create the kind of future we need.

Professor Rebecca Crane, PhD, Former Director, Centre for Mindfulness Research and Practice, Bangor University (UK)

*' As the authors remind us,
Ben Okri writes: 'Hospitality begins in the soul'.*

The words soul and soil are very close and this remarkable story of Trigonos explores both through a threefold lens that reveals how healing and dignity have been restored to the land and to the local community as well as those who visit from afar.'

Vivian Griffiths, Biodynamic Association
and Ruskin Mill Trust (UK)

"Thank you for writing a book on social business that aspires to inspire, not teach!

For those like me, who have had the privilege of spending time in the wonderful setting of Trigonos, this publication brings alive the importance of social business as a model for the future.

It also reveals the way in which the founder-directors worked so effectively alongside each other as a 'triumvirate' for over 20 years in a unique partnership."

Bulbul Baksi, Partnership Brokers Association